SCUNTHORPE
MURDERS

SCUNTHORPE
MURDERS

DOUGLAS WYNN

First published 2014

The History Press
The Mill, Brimscombe Port
Stroud, Gloucestershire, GL5 2QG
www.thehistorypress.co.uk

British Library Cataloguing in Publication Data.
A catalogue record for this book is available from the British Library.

ISBN 978 0 7509 5599 7

Typesetting and origination by The History Press
Printed in Great Britain

CONTENTS

Acknowledgements   6

Introduction   7

Case One   1921   The Mystery of the Reeds   10

Case Two   1936/7   A Shot in Time   25

Case Three   1945   Disaster Averted   41

Case Four   1953   Strange Mother Love   56

Case Five   1955   A Night Out with Menaces   71

Case Six   1966   A Question of Honour   86

Case Seven   1971   A Policeman's Lot   89

Case Eight   1971   Lethal Triangle   92

Case Nine   1973   A Continuing Mystery   97

Bibliography   112

ACKNOWLEDGEMENTS

I should like to thank the staff at the Scunthorpe Central Library, the Grimsby Reference Library and the Lincoln Central Library for their kind and helpful assistance. My grateful thanks are also due to Richard D'Arcy for help with research and for the loan of books and also to David Robinson for the loan of pictures from his collection. Grateful thanks also go to Rose Nicholson for images from the collection of the North Lincolnshire Museum and to Nick Tomlinson for images from the 'Picture the Past' collection. And to the editors of the *Scunthorpe Telegraph* and the *Grimsby Telegraph* for permission to use part of the publications under their control. Thanks also to Robert Hale Ltd for permission to use the picture of Norman Birkett, and to Hodder and Stoughton Ltd for permission to use the picture of Travers Humphreys. I should particularly like to thank Matilda Richards at The History Press for helpful advice during the writing of this book. And last but by no means least, to my dear wife Rosemary, for without her this book would never have been written.

All uncredited images are from my own collection.

INTRODUCTION

The name Scunthorpe comes from the Old Danish word 'Escumetorp' which meant 'Skuma's Homestead'. And indeed the original village was probably a Danish settlement on the limestone uplands known as the Lincoln Cliff, overlooking the Trent valley. Nineteenth-century maps show a rough line of five villages, nearly all with Danish names, running north and south and with less than a mile between each of them. They were from north to south: Crosby, Scunthorpe, Frodingham, Brumby and Ashby. Ashby was probably the biggest and it had the largest population until the census of 1871, when it was overtaken by Scunthorpe. This was because of the discovery of iron ore by Rowland Winn, who later became Lord St Oswald, on land belonging to his father near Scunthorpe. Iron ore was first mined in July 1860 and an iron works to which the ore could be processed was built in 1862. Other iron works followed, the last being Lysaght's Iron and Steel Works in 1911 – steel had first been manufactured in 1890. The workers for the new industry came from the agricultural community locally although skilled workers came from other areas like Sheffield. The work was hard and dangerous, particularly in the early days as the smelting process was often beset by explosions.

The fastest growth in population and prosperity came in Scunthorpe and Lord St Oswald provided a substantial town church, St John's. Scunthorpe was the first to reach urban district status in 1883. Frodingham and Brumby formed one unit until they joined with Ashby and became amalgamated with Scunthorpe in 1919. Then in 1936 Scunthorpe became a municipal borough, incorporating Ashby, Brumby, Frodingham and Crosby. The First World War increased the demand for steel, which led to even greater expansion. This continued through the Second World War until in 1974, the time of local government reorganisation, Scunthorpe was the largest town in North Lindsey. By then it had the huge Anchor Steel Works, a rail network linking to an ore terminal at the port of Immingham and a road network to the Humber Bridge, south to Lincoln, east to Grimsby and west to the Midlands. But the future was not as bright as it looked. In 1981 it was decided to close all local mines and only use iron ore from abroad; local ore contained only 20 per cent iron whereas imported ore contained 60–70 per cent. There were and are proven reserves of iron ore beneath the Scunthorpe area, but it remains cheaper to use imports. However, today the steel industry is still the major employer in the town, the largest employer being Tata Steel.

Apart from iron and steel there are other industries. Some are engineering works associated with steel, but there is also a food industry involved in production, distribution and retailing, which employs immigrant labour on a large scale, mostly from Poland and Slovakia. The steel industry has also employed immigrant labour, particularly in the boom era of the late 1970s, and these came mainly from the Middle East.

Because Scunthorpe is a relatively new town, the councils were able to plan the development carefully and to use the historical fact of five nuclei to create plenty of open spaces between them. It has justly been called the Industrial Garden Town.

Notable people from the town include:

- Daren Bett,
  BBC Weather presenter.
- Ian Collins, radio presenter
  born in the town.
- Howard Devoto and
  Ian Mathews, singers.
- Reece Mastin, singer
  and winner of *X-Factor*
  Australia in 2011.
- David Plowright,
  television producer.
- Peter D. Robinson, Archbishop
  of the United Episcopal Church
  of North America. (Was born
  in Scunthorpe but grew up in
  nearby Barton-upon-Humber.)
- Graham Taylor, former
  England football manager.

St John's church.

But even a garden town has its share of murders and mayhem. This book contains a selection of cases where an individual was charged with murder, but not always convicted, except for one. The disappearance of a Scunthorpe schoolgirl in 1973 is now regarded as murder, but no body has been found and no one has been charged with the crime.

Murder, the ultimate crime and the cause of appalling suffering, continues to fascinate. The discovery of the skeletons of two young children in 1921, for example, shocked the town and resulted in a trial which added more surprises. Then there was the woman who shot her husband after his night out on the tiles. The dreadful murder of an elderly woman, which was thought to be the work of a maniac, resulted in the calling in of Scotland Yard detectives and the case threw up more surprises than anybody could possibly have expected. What about the respectable middle-aged wife? Could she be capable of slaughtering her teenage daughter? And in another intriguing case, did the quiet young man kill a prostitute? In Scunthorpe's history a fight in a steelworks also turned to murder and a local policeman was accused of killing his wife. And the suspect in a double murder barricaded himself in a house and held the police at bay for many hours. All these stories show the variability of the human psyche and that the motives for violent and lethal action are many and varied.

Douglas Wynn

CASE ONE   1921

THE MYSTERY OF THE REEDS

Suspect: Charles Wolfe
Age: 30
Charge: Murder

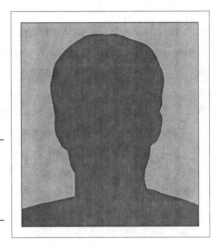

It was in the early morning of Tuesday, 15 November 1921 that farmworker Frederick Rimes was cutting reeds in a low-lying valley near the railway viaduct at Brumby. The area was usually very wet and boggy, but it had been a dry summer and the ground was less damp than usual. Nevertheless the reeds were over 7 feet high and very thickly clumped in places, so it was a lonely spot, frequented by very few people. When he saw something white on the ground in front of him he stopped working and bent to examine it. Then a ray of sunlight caught it and he jumped back in alarm. It was a small skull. He took a closer look and saw that it was not from an animal; it was round and undoubtedly human. The skull of a small child.

As he looked closer he could see bones scattered about. This was no sheep carcase or even a dog. This was murder! He rushed back to Rowbottom Farm, to the farmer who had employed him, and burst out with his news. The farmer himself went to inspect the find and then cycled to Scunthorpe police station to report the discovery. At 10 a.m. that Tuesday, Superintendent Johnson, Sergeant Sharman and several police constables cycled out to the spot indicated by the farmer. What they found there surprised and shocked them. Though the bones had been scattered somewhat by animals, it was obvious enough that there were two separate individuals, one smaller than the other. But little else remained. No flesh adhered to the bones, so they must have been there some time, but there were some scraps of clothing that might help to identify the bodies. There was a girl's hat, boots, jacket and a pocket handkerchief.

When Dr Bellamy, the police doctor, arrived he opined that they were the skeletons of two children: the older one possibly 6 or 7 and the younger 2 or 3. He wasn't able to positively determine the sex of the children right away, though from the clothing at least one looked to be female. He also estimated that they had been on the ground for at least two months.

'This was murder!'

Superintendent Johnson considered that the two children might have been local and had wandered off, become disorientated, couldn't find their way back home and so perished in that lonely spot. But if that was so, why had nobody reported them missing? And he could recall no notices asking for information about missing children. No, their disappearance was decidedly suspicious. He therefore reported the find to the local press and asked for information from anyone who had heard of children going missing over the last two months or so.

Among the reports that he received was one from Mrs Kate Martin living in Fenton Street. She reported that she had started a job as a housekeeper in March, working for a Charles Wolfe. He had two children, Grace who

Scunthorpe Viaduct. (Courtesy of David Robinson)

was 6 and young Herbert who was 3, and Martin looked after them and their clothing. In July, Wolfe obtained a position as a steamroller driver for a firm in Manchester. On a Friday early in August, he sent Martin a letter asking her to send the children to him by train to Ardwick Station on the Great Central Railway. But she was unable to do this and on the following Friday he cycled to Scunthorpe. On the Monday, she dressed Grace in a white hat, brown coat and white socks and Wolfe took both children away, telling her that he was trying to get the children into a home. He left at about 2.30 p.m. that day with the children and returned alone at about 9.30 p.m., saying that a nurse had met the children in Doncaster and they had gone with her.

Martin was able to give the police Wolfe's address, since he had written to her several times since he had left. And on Thursday, 17 November, Inspector Metcalf from the Scunthorpe Police travelled north and interviewed Charles Wolfe where he was living at Crooklands, Preston Richard, Westmoreland (now part of Cumbria). He repeated that he left his children with a nurse at Doncaster Station. When he was asked where they

Fenton Street today.

were now he said he didn't know, but suspected that they were out of the country and in France. The inspector said he was not satisfied with Wolfe's statement and brought him back to Scunthorpe where he was remanded in custody until the following Monday.

The inquest on the two skeletons was opened in Scunthorpe on Saturday, 19 November before coroner Mr G.E. Davy and a jury. The court was crowded, as the discovery of the skeletons had caused a sensation in the town. Wolfe, whose name was given as Charles Herbert Wolfe and whose age was 30, was present, as were his father, mother, sister, brother and sister-in-law, who all lived in the town. The coroner told Wolfe that he would have an opportunity of giving evidence if he wished and he answered, 'Righto.'

Frederick Rimes gave evidence of finding the remains and Sergeant Benson produced photographs he had taken of the crime scene. Superintendent Johnson reported going to see the skeletons at the place they were found. In answer to a question from one of the jurors, he said that the position of the bodies was a kind of inverted V, with the head of the female towards the feet of the younger child. It appeared to him to be a natural position and he said it was possible that they might have died in their sleep. Sergeant Sharman produced the clothing that had been found by the bodies, but said that there were no laundry marks on any of the clothing. He also produced some brown hair that had been adhering to the skull of the older child.

Dr Bellamy had collected all the bones and had arranged them into two bodies. He was able to tell the jury that there were few bones missing and to confirm that they came from two individuals; one older child

Charles Wolfe.
(Courtesy of John Young)

13

aged 6 or thereabouts and one from a much younger child of 2 or 3. There was practically no tissue left on the bones and nothing to indicate any violence or cause of death. He estimated that death had taken place some two months before, although it was very difficult to pinpoint the exact time.

Next into the witness box was Kate Martin. She repeated the evidence she had given the police and when she was shown the clothes which had been found near the bodies, she said she was sure that they were worn by Grace when she last saw her. She also said that she had seen Wolfe later that evening when he had told her that the girl would become a nun and the boy a sailor, when he grew older.

At this Wolfe spoke up. 'Tell me if you did not suggest many times to get the children away, as you could not stand the slander being put about. Answer me straight lass.'

Martin replied that she had suggested he might try and get the children away as they were so dirty.

Wolfe put another question. 'What did I look like when I walked into the house that Monday night? Was I excited?'

'No,' replied Martin. 'I don't think you were.'

Grace Wolfe.
(Courtesy of John Young)

The next day she said Wolfe returned to Manchester. Further evidence of the clothing was given by Gertrude Martin, Mrs Martin's daughter, who had lived with her in the Fenton Street house. She said that she helped to get the children dressed on that fateful day. She had shortened the elastic on the girl's hat by putting a knot in it. And it was the same knot that was on the girl's hat produced in court.

When the court adjourned for lunch Wolfe was visited by his father and mother. After lunch evidence was given by a coalman who said that he saw Wolfe with his children at about 6.30 p.m. that Monday on Althorpe Bank, which is on the opposite side of the River Trent from Scunthorpe. This was the first indication that Wolfe's story of taking the children to Doncaster that night might not be true. Inspector Metcalf gave evidence of Wolfe telling him that the children were in a home in France. The inspector then told him that it was possible he might be charged with the wilful murder of his two children. Wolfe replied, 'Have my two poor babies been found then?' The coroner adjourned the inquiry at that point until Tuesday, 29 November. When he was asked if he would like to give evidence Wolfe said, 'I reserve my defence. I have nothing to say, only that I am innocent of anything.'

Herbert Wolfe.
(Courtesy of John Young)

When the inquest was resumed on Tuesday, 29 November the coroner's court was again very crowded and a murmur of anticipation went round the room as Mrs Wolfe, Wolfe's estranged wife, went in the witness box. The coroner told her that she need not give evidence unless she wished to do so, but the jury would be glad to hear it if she wished to speak. Mrs Wolfe, however, intimated that she did not wish to speak. Thereupon the coroner read the following signed statement, given previously to Detective Smith:

I am the wife of Charles Wolfe and I reside at 2 Clare Street, Burnley. I was married to Charles Wolfe on the 26 June 1915, at the Westgate Congregational Church, Burnley. Two children were born of the marriage, Grace Mary was born on 24 August 1915, and Charles Herbert was born on 20 March 1918. After the marriage I resided with my father and the prisoner, who was employed as a steam road engine driver for a firm of the name Norman E. Box, contractor, Manchester and was away from home a good deal. He visited me on an average of once a fortnight. After about six months I removed to 49 Holsby Street, Ardwick, Manchester where we resided together for about four years and during that time he constantly complained about the home and the children not having proper attention.

About the end of 1919 I was prosecuted at Manchester for neglect of children by the NSPCC and was discharged on condition that I returned to my father and from then my husband took charge of the children. I returned to Burnley to reside with my father and my husband went to reside along with the two children with his parents at Scunthorpe, Lincolnshire. I did not see my husband again until he visited me at my father's house, in August 1920, where I am still residing. My husband informed me that my daughter Grace Mary was dead. On the occasion of that visit he only stayed with me a few minutes and made no request for me to return with him. I have not seen him since. About September of this year I received the attached letter from him which was answered by my father. I have not seen the children since the time I parted from my husband in Manchester.

The letter which Mrs Wolfe had received contained the following passages:

Madam, I am writing this letter to you to ask if you will take and look after your two children for a while, until such time that I can make a fresh home for them? I am giving you this one chance to redeem yourself ... To tell the truth I wish they and I were dead, as I am fed up of life completely ... The only thing you will have to watch is being strict with them and learn them to keep themselves clean, as they are now. If you do not accept, this will be the last chance of you ever seeing us again or coming together ... It is urgent that you accept and take them on Saturday. After that it will be too late, as where the children are the home belongs to the housekeeper and she is taking everything away.

The coroner having summed up evidence for the jury, they retired to consider their verdict. After a few minutes they returned and their foreman said that they were unanimously of the opinion that the

Magistrates' court, 1960s. (Courtesy of North Lincolnshire Museum Service Image Archive)

identity of the two children had been proved by strong circumstantial evidence and that the children had been murdered by their father on 29 August. The coroner then committed Wolfe to take his trial at the next Lincolnshire Assizes. Wolfe, who had stood while the corner addressed him replied, 'Yes, sir.' Both the coroner and the jury expressed appreciation of the Lincolnshire Police for their promptitude and efficiency in dealing with the case.

The following morning (30 November) Wolfe was brought before magistrate Mr J.G. Cutts and Superintendent Johnson asked for a further remand for eight days to enable the whole of the evidence to be submitted to the public prosecutor. Wolfe was then brought before the magistrates Mr T. Cliff, Mr J. Fletcher and Mrs Hornsby, at the magistrates' court in Scunthorpe, on Thursday, 8 December. Mr Peevour appeared for the Director of Public Prosecutions and the court was as usual very crowded. Wolfe entered the dock with a smile on his face and looked round at the people in the court. As usual his family were in attendance. He was allowed to sit between two warders.

Mr Peevour reviewed the evidence that had been given at the inquest. He drew attention to when Wolfe was seen walking along the Althorpe Bank at 6.30 p.m., pointing out that the train service from Scunthorpe to Doncaster would not have allowed him, leaving his home in Scunthorpe at 2.30 p.m., to be back by 6.30 p.m.

Kate Martin and her daughter Gertrude were called and repeated the evidence they had given at the inquest. At the end of Gertrude's evidence Wolfe asked her, 'Are you positive you saw me at 9.30 on that Monday evening?'

'Yes,' replied the witness.

'At my house?'

'Yes.'

'Very good. Thank you.'

A new witness appeared at this stage. He was William Delamore of Althorpe Bank. He said that he knew Wolfe well and indeed Wolfe had been with him at Delamore's house the Sunday before the disappearance of the two children. He had a drink there and was given some apples to

Bank End, Althorpe, looking east, 1920s. (Courtesy of North Lincolnshire Museum Service Image Archive)

take home and when he left he said he was going home to his two children. William Delamore saw Wolfe again the next day. He was on the other side of Althorpe walking towards the village and he had two children with him, a boy and a girl. They stopped to talk. Wolfe had said he was going to catch the 6 p.m. train to Doncaster from Althorpe, but it was 6.30 p.m. when Delamore saw him. Wolfe said he had missed the train and asked if there was another. Delamore told him that the next one was not until 8.45 p.m. and Wolfe appeared put out by this, but carried on walking with the two children towards Althorpe.

This evidence was more or less confirmed by another witness, John Houghton. He said that he knew Wolfe very well and that at one time they were fellow workmen. He wasn't sure about the exact date he had seen Wolfe, but thought it was near the end of August or the beginning of September. He thought it was about 6 p.m. when he saw Wolfe with two children near Althorpe. Wolfe told him that the two children were his. Wolfe then went off with the children towards Althorpe and Scunthorpe. The usual way for people on foot to get to Scunthorpe was along the footpath by the railway.

Another new witness followed John Houghton. She was Alice Cockburn and she gave her address as Concrete Houses, Endmore, near Kendal. She said that she had known Wolfe about two months, when he was working on the road outside her house. They got quite friendly and used to go out together and during conversations she had with him he told her that he had two children, a girl of 6 and a boy of 3, who had been adopted by someone living in France.

Thomas Smith, who was the father of Mrs Wolfe, confirmed that Wolfe had married his daughter and that two children, a boy and a girl, had been born to them. He also confirmed that he had replied to a letter Wolfe had sent his wife about the custody of the two children. Inspector Metcalf also gave evidence of the arrest of Wolfe.

When the chairman of the magistrates, Talbot Cliff, asked Wolfe if he had anything to say before judgement was passed, he said, 'No,' and reserved his defence. He was then committed for trial at the next Lincolnshire Assizes. Wolfe was smiling when left the dock. He shook hands with his father-in-law and patted him on the head.

Lincolnshire Assize Court.

The trial opened on Friday, 3 March 1922 at the Crown Court in Lincoln Castle. It was the most sensational case that had come before the courts for many years and the court was packed. Extra benches had to be brought in to accommodate the large number of reporters who attended and accommodation usually used by instructing solicitors was turned over to the press. Wolfe appeared in the dock a few minutes before 10.30 a.m. He appeared calm and collected and answered the questions put to him about the jury by Mr G.P. Bancroft, the Clerk to the Assizes, in a clear firm voice. He was allowed to object, if he wished, to a certain number of jurors, but he only asked one juror while being sworn to hold the testament book up.

Mr Justice Horridge officiated and the prosecution was in the hands of Mr T. Hollis Walker KC (King's Counsel) and Mr Sinclair Johnson, while Wolfe was defended by Mr P.E. Sandlands. Walker outlined the case against the prisoner, suggesting that on the evidence there could be but one inference as to what had happened; that the prisoner took the children to the spot indicated, killed them there and left them. The judge, after this statement, said that it was his duty to tell the jury that there was no occasion to prove the actual killing of the children. If the inference was that the children had been left to die, it was clearly murder.

Frederick Rimes, Superintendent Johnson, Dr John Bellamy, Kate Martin and her daughter Gertrude all repeated the evidence they had given at the committal proceedings. William Delamore was unable to attend because of illness so his deposition was read by Mr G.E. Davy, Clerk to the Scunthorpe Magistrates. This was followed by John Houghton and Alice Coburn. A new witness was Louis Ayre, chief clerk at the booking office at Scunthorpe Station. He said that no children's tickets were issued on Sunday, 29 August for the 2.22 p.m. train, nor for the 4.41 p.m. train to Doncaster. There was no way a person who had missed the 4.41 train could get from Althorpe to Doncaster and back to Scunthorpe the same night. Thomas Smith, who was a widower and the father of Mrs Wolfe, gave evidence of the birth of the two children and by cross-examination of the witness Mr Sandlands was able to introduce the evidence of Mrs Wolfe, which had been presented at the inquest.

Crowle Station, 1923. (Courtesy of North Lincolnshire Museum Service Image Archive)

This closed the case for the prosecution. Sandlands, opening the case for the defence, put his client in the witness box at once. Wolfe corroborated the evidence of the last witness and said that since his wife had been charged with neglecting her children and they had been put in his care he had sole charge of them. He had shared a home with his mother and father at Scunthorpe and with a Mr and Mrs Abbott and their children (Mrs Abbott being his sister). In December 1920 the Abbotts left to get a home of their own and in February 1921 his parents also left to share a home with his brother Tom. Wolfe then advertised for a housekeeper and engaged Mrs Kate Martin who was separated from her husband. Her daughter Gertrude also came to live in the house in Fenton Street and helped to look after the children.

Wolfe continued to work in Scunthorpe until he was offered a job with a firm in Manchester as a steamroller driver working on the roads, a firm he had worked for before. It was in the first week of July that he went to Manchester, but he continued to pay the rent and sent money for the children's upkeep. Continuing his evidence he said that he was anxious to have his children nearer to him and he wrote to Martin asking her to send the children to him by rail. He also wrote to his wife on Monday, 24 August (the letter which was placed in evidence at the inquest). The children did not arrive and Martin sent a telegram saying it was too late to send the children. On the following Sunday he cycled to Scunthorpe and he admitted that he told Martin he was going to take the children to a home, but he had no home ready for them to go to.

The next day, Monday, he took the children out at about 2 p.m. He admitted that he told Martin he was going to take them to Doncaster, but he did not go there. He went to the station and took a train to Crowle – Crowle is about 9.6 kilometres (6 miles) west of Scunthorpe and 7.2 kilometres (4½ miles) from Althorpe. He took one single for himself and one for the little girl. He got out at Crowle and walked back with them towards Althorpe along the canal bank by the side of the railway. He stopped at a house to ask if this was the right way to Althorpe and a woman told he was going in the wrong direction. He had come some miles out of his way and had to retrace his steps. Sometimes he carried the young boy but mostly they all walked. When they were near

Althorpe he saw Delamore. It was his intention to catch the train but Delamore told him it had gone. He went up past the station at Althorpe with the children, over the level crossing and on the bridge over the Trent. They went past some houses and a public house and went along a pathway. When they had gone some way along the pathway they sat down to rest. The children were very tired as it was three hours after their bedtime and so they went to sleep.

'What came into your head then?' asked Sandlands.

'At first, while they were asleep, the thought came to me that if I left them there asleep, someone would find them before night and that would be the means of getting them into a home or an institution.'

Wolfe went back to Scunthorpe alone, calling at Mrs Martin's mother's house, where he knew Martin would be, and together they went back to Fenton Street. He said that he had taken the children because Mrs Martin had refused to look after them after the Saturday.

He was cross-examined severely by Walker who asked him about the lies he had told Martin. He got Wolfe to admit that he had told an adoption society that he was out of work whereas he had never been out of work in Manchester. He also asked him why he never made any enquiries about the children. Even the judge was moved to ask him, 'Did it not occur to you that leaving the children near the footpath at eight o'clock at night, there might be serious consequences?'

Wolfe replied, 'No, sir.'

'Do you seriously mean that?'

'Yes sir.'

Soon after this Wolfe appeared to collapse. He was given water and examined by the prison doctor who told the judge that he was suffering from palpitations and faintness and asked if the prisoner could be allowed to go below and lie down for some time. The judge agreed and Wolfe was assisted down the steps of the dock to the cells. Ten or fifteen minutes later he returned to answer a few questions by the judge. Both counsels then addressed the jury and the judge summed up. He said that the law was that a verdict of wilful murder ought not to be returned unless the jury were satisfied beyond reasonable doubt that Wolfe did kill the children by putting them in a position where they would not be found. If, on the other hand, Wolfe had put them in such a position that they might possibly be found, and the jury thought that the act was gross cruel neglect, then he would be guilty of manslaughter.

The jury retired for three quarters of an hour before returning to deliver a verdict of guilty of manslaughter. Addressing the prisoner, Justice Horridge said that the jury had taken an extremely merciful view of the case. The sentence was seven years' penal servitude. The verdict and the sentence surprised many people. Some thought that he was lucky not to face the death sentence. The hope is that he had learned his lesson.

CASE TWO 1936/7

A SHOT
IN TIME

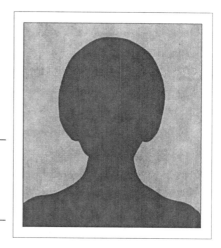

Suspect:	Doris Teesdale
Age:	28
Charge:	Murder

It was a Sunday evening in Scunthorpe, just after Christmas, when Mrs Doris Teesdale said to her husband: 'Are you going out again?' It was rather a rhetorical question since Cecil Teesdale, 28, was obviously getting changed and had brought the car round to the front of the bungalow.

'It looks like it, doesn't it?'

'Where are you going then?'

High Street. (Courtesy of David Robinson)

'Just out. I don't know where it will be until I get there.'

'You're going to those friends of yours in Grimsby, aren't you?' But Cecil Teesdale did not reply. Doris tried again. 'Take me with you.'

Her husband laughed. 'It's no use you going, you're not broadminded enough.'

The Teesdales were a well-known family in Scunthorpe. Cecil Teesdale had a thriving butchery business in the High Street and he and his wife Doris, who was also 28, lived at Comforts Avenue. They had been married for nine years and had a baby, but had lost one son some years before. Doris Vanda Ursula Teesdale came from the Wolsey family in Lincoln and had met her future husband when he was living and working in Lincoln. But it cannot be said that the marriage was a happy one, especially lately. Doris complained bitterly that her husband frequently left her alone while he went off with his friends, often with other women as well. In fact, he had boasted to her that he kissed other women. She was very lonely and depressed, particularly this Christmas. They had a midday meal together on Christmas Day, but in the afternoon he went off to visit his mother. Then on Boxing Day, when she had arranged a party in the evening, he did not come home till 10 p.m.

It was on Sunday, 27 December 1936, that he went off with his friends. Doris went to bed at about 11 p.m., thinking Cecil would be home by midnight. She tossed and turned in bed worrying about what he might be up to. Midnight came and went. No Cecil. She began to think that he might have had an accident in his car. Eventually she fell into a troubled sleep. It wasn't until after 9 a.m. the next morning that Cecil finally arrived home. According to the maid, Amy Kirby, he came in the back door and through into the scullery, then straight into the bedroom. 'Good morning darling,' he said cheerily, and went into the bathroom. Doris got up and began dressing. She too went into the bathroom and followed her husband into the dining room. He was just sitting down to his breakfast.

'Where have you been all night?' she said.

'Just out.'

'Yes, but you must have been in someone's house to stay all night.'

'Oh, no one that you know.'

'That's all very well, but you can surely tell me where you've been.'

The maid, who had shut the door to the scullery after Doris had gone into the dining room, could hear the quarrel but couldn't make out a lot of what was said. She heard some footsteps, which she recognised as Doris's, leave the dining room and cross the tiled floor of the hall. Then the footsteps returned to the dining room. The quarrelling continued. But this time rather more loudly. She heard Cecil say, 'Stop fooling!'

'I'm not fooling!' came the shouted reply.

Soon after this came the sound of a shot, followed by a crash and then groans. Amy went to the door into the dining room and was met by Doris in the doorway. She could see past her mistress into the dining room, where Cecil was lying on the floor between the table and a settee, and groaning.

'Fetch the doctor!' said Doris.

Amy turned and rushed out of the house. There was a dental surgeon, a James Vogwell, who lived only a few doors away and she went and knocked on his door. It was opened by the Revd Roland Thompson, a Congregational minister from Goole who was staying with James Vogwell. She told them what had happened and all three hurried back to the house in Comforts Avenue. When Vogwell entered the house he noticed the sharp smell of a recently fired revolver. Doris Teesdale was in a very excitable state. She rushed towards him saying, 'I have shot him. I never intended to. It was only to frighten him. You know that, don't you Mr Vogwell?'

'Where is he?'

'I have shot him. I never intended to. It was only to frighten him.'

Doris Teesdale pushed open the door into the dining room with her left hand then put the hand to her face. Vogwell went in and found Cecil Teesdale lying on the floor. He appeared to have a hole in the left side of his jacket and was obviously injured. But he was also conscious. When he saw the dentist bending over him he muttered, 'Look after her, it was only a blank.'

Vogwell enquired if an ambulance had been ordered and, learning that a doctor had been summoned, he returned to his house and phoned the police. Then he came back to house on Comforts Avenue. Meanwhile the minister was trying to comfort Doris. She said to him, 'I have never handled a gun before in my life. Why did it happen? Why did he have them about? When he fell I thought he was joking. I would never harm him. I worshipped him.'

Cecil Teesdale also said to the Revd Thompson: 'Look after her. She will do away with herself. They are only blanks. I will not go to hospital.' But he soon lapsed into unconsciousness. When Dr Thomas Cullam arrived he examined Cecil and realised that he had a bullet wound in his side. Cullam arranged for him to be taken to hospital, where he was seen by Dr William Smith, the resident surgeon at Scunthorpe's War Memorial Hospital. Cecil was suffering from shock and a puncture wound just at the edge of the ribs. Dr Smith ordered an X-ray and this showed a bullet lodged in the right buttock. There was also evidence that the bowel was injured in two places where the bullet had passed through. He decided to operate immediately.

The police, in the shape of Police Constable Warren, had arrived soon after the doctor, and the policeman accompanied Cecil to hospital in the ambulance. He also phoned his superiors and Inspector Herbert Cook and Detective Sergeant Brewster arrived soon after. Later the detective

Comforts Avenue today.

sergeant went to the hospital and was given the bullet that had been taken from Cecil Teesdale during the operation. The sergeant also asked his wife, Mrs Lillian Brewster, to go to Comforts Avenue and sit with Doris Teesdale because he feared she might try and commit suicide. Lillian stayed with Doris most of that day. During their conversations Doris said:

I am so lonely. If he had only taken me with him this would never have happened. I would not hurt him for the world. I love him so. I only meant to frighten him. I only shot to go by the side of him.

She also described the actual shooting:

He was there, I was here. I shot! I don't know, it just went off. He fell to the floor. I said: 'Get up Cecil; stop joking.' He began to moan and I sent for a doctor at once. I don't know anything about firearms. I don't know how to use them.

Doris Teesdale.
(Courtesy of John Young)

Later that day she was arrested by Inspector Cook and charged with attempting to murder her husband. She appeared before a special police court that afternoon and Superintendent Dolby asked for a remand in custody until Wednesday. Cook said that when he read over the charge to Doris she made no reply. She was duly remanded. When she appeared before the magistrates on Wednesday she was wearing a small green hat and a fur coat. She looked very pale and her eyes were puffed as if she had been weeping. She was defended by local solicitor Mr J.T. Lewis, who protested vigorously to the magistrates about the standard of accommodation for women in the Scunthorpe area. The chairman of the magistrates asked him to send in his protest in writing and after the hearing he himself went to inspect the facilities for women at the Scunthorpe police station. Superintendent Dolby asked for a further remand in custody until the next Wednesday and Doris was ordered to be taken to Hull Prison, where they had better facilities for women prisoners.

The following Friday, Cecil Teesdale was reported to be very ill in hospital, though it was stated that he had had a comfortable night. But he died in hospital just after midnight on Sunday morning, in the presence of his relatives. He had made no further statement. The inquest was opened by the coroner Mr G.E. Davy on Monday, 4 January. Mr Lewis represented Doris Teesdale and the family were represented by Mr A.A. Collins. The coroner proposed to take only identification evidence and medical evidence and then adjourn the enquiry. Mr Harold Teesdale, the father of the dead man, who lived in Messingham Road, Ashby, said that he had seen his son when he was taken to hospital on the Monday and had seen him every day until the day of his death. The coroner said, 'On behalf of everyone here I would like to express our sincere sympathy with you.'

Dr William Smith said that after Cecil Teesdale had had the operation he progressed satisfactorily for a few days until peritonitis set in, which he died from early on Sunday morning. At the request of the coroner he had performed a post-mortem examination in the presence of Dr Russell Stamford the day before the court. He reported that there was an external opening due to the bullet wound. The wound was in the left flank and the eleventh rib was fractured by the bullet about

Cecil Teesdale.
(Courtesy of John Young)

2 inches from the top. The bullet had passed through the abdomen, penetrating the bowels in two places and came to rest in the right buttock. It had been found with its nose pointing upwards, probably because of striking the rib. The bullet had been extracted. He said that the liver was congested with peritonitis and this had been the actual cause of death.

The corner reviewed the evidence and said that the jury had heard a charge had been made in respect of the injuries and he proposed to say nothing further. He adjourned the inquest for a month. On the following Wednesday, Superintendent Dolby reported to the magistrates that the charge was now murder and asked for a further remand in custody to Hull Prison until a date could be fixed for a full hearing of the charge. After some discussion this was fixed at 22 January. Doris Teesdale, who had been brought from Hull by car, was wearing a bottle-green fur-trimmed coat, fur collar and close-fitting green hat. The journey back to Hull was made by police car. The funeral of Cecil Walter Teesdale took place on the same afternoon at Brumby Cemetery. It was preceded by a service at St Lawrence church, Frodingham.

It was reported that on the Tuesday following the committal proceedings, there would be a public auction of all the household effects of the Teesdale's home. The auctioneers, Messrs. Joseph R. Trafford, had received instructions from the executors of Cecil Teesdale's will to sell all the household furniture and effects, including the 28-horsepower sports car. The sale would take place at the house.

The committal proceedings opened at the police court on Friday, 22 January. Mr. E.G. Robey appeared for the Director of Public Prosecutions and Mr Lewis represented Mrs Doris Teesdale. Lewis made a formal application for legal aid for the prisoner as a poor person. He understood that a defence fund was being raised in the town, but he had no idea what amount would be forthcoming.

Robey outlined the case, saying that a large Spanish revolver had been discharged at Cecil Teesdale and he subsequently died in hospital. The firing of the revolver was a voluntary act by the prisoner and was intended either to kill him or cause him grievous bodily harm. Amy Kirby was his first witness. She said that she had been employed by the Teesdales for nine weeks. She described what she saw and heard when Cecil came

War Memorial Hospital, 1930–39. (Courtesy of North Lincolnshire Museum Service Image Archive)

home that Sunday morning and subsequently when she went to fetch Vogwell and Thompson.

Then Robey asked her if it was the first time she had heard a gun go off in the house. She said that it was not and described an occasion three weeks before, at about 6 p.m. Shown a photograph of the dining room, she said that when she went into the room after hearing the shot on that occasion, Cecil was sitting on the left-hand side and Doris was sitting facing him. She had a gun, which Amy recognised as the one produced in court. Soon after she had gone into the room, Cecil left the house. The next day Doris showed her a place on the floor where the bullet had gone in. Cross-examined by Lewis, she admitted that Doris was a good wife and, apart from occasional tiffs, the couple got on well together.

Vogwell gave his evidence, saying that he had seen a revolver when he went into the dining room, on the left-hand side on a chair. He was followed by Revd Roland Thompson, Dr Cullan, Dr Smith and Police Constable Warren. Then Ernest Sidney Teesdale entered the witness box. He described himself as a butcher of Messingham Road. He said that Cecil had been his brother and had owned the revolver produced in court for about ten years. Cecil also possessed a small dummy pistol of the automatic type.

He was followed by George William Taylor, who was also a butcher and had known Cecil and his wife for many years. He described the party that he and Teesdale had gone to that Saturday night and said that the last time he saw him was when he dropped him off at his home on Sunday morning.

Cerina Ann Rowbottom of Kirton Lindsey said she had been employed as a maid by the Teesdales. She frequently heard quarrels between them and Doris told her that her husband was keeping late hours and going out with other women. She also saw Cecil smack his wife on two occasions. During the time she worked there, she found that Doris was a good mother, fond of her home, kind to her husband and devoted to her child.

Detective Sergeant Brewster described how he took the following statement from the accused:

If only he had taken me with him it would not have happened, but he only just came in. I shot at him to scare him. I love him too much to hurt him. I am so lonely. He leaves me hours upon hours.

The sergeant also found sixteen 0.455 live cartridges and three empty cases in the Teesdale's sitting room. Cross-examined by Lewis, he said that Doris was not in a very fit condition, but in his opinion was not too upset.

Lewis said, 'I put it to you that what she said was not, "I shot *at him* to scare him" but "I shot to scare him".' The sergeant replied that he put down what she said and read it over to her and that she had agreed with it.

'Was there anyone else present at the time?'

'No.'

Dr Henry Holden, Director of Forensic Science at Nottingham University, said he had examined the clothing worn by Cecil. There was no scorching on the cloth and he deduced that the shot had not been fired at point blank range. In his opinion it had travelled horizontally. George Carter, who was a staff chemist working under Dr Holden, tested the revolver produced in court. By firing another bullet from it and comparing his bullet with the one found in Cecil, he concluded that both bullets had both been fired

from the same weapon. Walter
Speckley, a gun maker from
West Bridgeford, Nottingham,
said that the revolver was an old
one, with a normal trigger pull of 5¾lbs (2.6kg).
It would be impossible to discharge it accidently,
but there was no safety catch. To discharge a bullet
it would have to be placed in the left-hand chamber of
the revolver. This rotated when the trigger was pulled.

The case for the prosecution was completed at 4.35 p.m. Lewis then submitted that his client had no case to answer and the magistrates duly retired. They returned shortly afterwards and sent Doris Teesdale for trial at the next Lincolnshire Assizes.

The trial took place at Lincoln on Monday, 8 February 1937, before Mr Justice Humphreys. Mr Richard O'Sullivan K.C. and Mr J.P. Stimson prosecuted, with Mr Norman Birkett K.C. and Mr Winning defending. Before 7 a.m. there was a queue (of mainly women) waiting for the gates of the castle to open and special buses had been run from Scunthorpe to accommodate the many people who wanted to attend the trial. When the main gates under the ramparts of the castle were opened, people streamed across the lawns to reach the court doors and the public gallery was filled within a few minutes.

When Mr O'Sullivan opened the case for the prosecution the revolver was on the table beside him. He outlined the circumstances leading up to the shooting, finishing with the remarks that he thought the case was one of manslaughter. He then called the witnesses who had been examined at the committal proceedings. When Dr Smith gave his evidence and produced the bullet extracted from Cecil Teesdale, the judge asked to see it. After examining it closely he gave it to a court official saying, 'Let the jury see the bullet so they can see the size of it.' The judge intervened in the evidence of Cecil's brother, asking him if he visited Cecil after his brother was married.

'Very seldom,' said Ernest Teesdale.

'But you lived in Scunthorpe, didn't you?'

'Yes,' replied Ernest Teesdale.

Taylor then described the party at Pacey's house in Grimsby. He said that there were two women there and the party broke up in the early hours of the morning. He said that he saw one of the women later in the passage at Pacey's house.

Mr O'Sullivan asked him, 'Do you know where the lady passed the night?'

'No,' replied Taylor, 'but it wasn't with me!'

This caused some laughter in court, which was severely rebuked by the judge.

Mr Birkett took up the questioning. 'What time did the lady leave the party?'

'As far as I can say, between three and four in the morning.'

'Did the other lady go as well?'

'They all went out together. The two ladies, Teesdale, a young man and myself.'

'Did you and Teesdale go back to bed at Pacey's house?'

'I did, Teesdale lay on the couch.'

Brumby Cemetery. (Courtesy of North Lincolnshire Museum Service Image Archive)

When the case for the Crown closed, Mrs Doris Teesdale went into the witness box. Mr Birkett first asked her, 'Was there any time when in consequence of the conduct of your husband with other women, of staying out late, you had in mind doing him any harm?'

'Never. I wanted to get him back as a husband.'

Birkett then took her through the events of that Saturday night and Sunday morning. After describing her conversation with Cecil in the dining room, and her asking where he had been, she said: 'He did not want to tell me and after talking to him for a few minutes I went to get

Travers Humphreys.
(Courtesy of Hodder & Stoughton)

the gun. I went to the front bedroom for the gun which was always kept between the bed and the mattress.'

'Why did you go to get the gun at all?'

'I had no idea of firing it, but I thought it would just scare him into telling me where he had been that night.'

'Had you any knowledge of firearms?'

'None whatsoever. I have never seen one loaded or discharged.'

'Did you know whether it was loaded?'

'No, I did not. When he told me to stop fooling and I said I was not fooling, he said, "Oh well it does not matter. You cannot do any harm with that it is only loaded with blanks."'

Birkett then said, 'There came a moment when there was a shot. Tell the jury how it came to be fired.'

'He still persisted in not telling me. I fired just to scare him. I fired it off more to the side of him. I thought it would be between him and the table. I was at one corner of the table and he was at the other. I think I aimed more to the left side.'

Birkett recalled the occasion three weeks before when the first shot was fired in the dining room. Doris remembered that on that night her husband had come home at about 4 a.m. After lunch he went to sleep in a chair. They did not quarrel, but she told him that she did not think it right that he should come home so early in the morning. He replied that he knew she was all right and was asleep in bed. She then told him that she was afraid because the garage door was open and people could see that his car was not there and anyone would know that he was not in the house. It was usual to keep a considerable amount of money in the house at times.

Cecil then said, 'You don't want to be afraid. You want to get that gun.' He went through to the bedroom and fetched the gun. 'You can't hurt people, they are only blanks.'

Norman Birkett. (Courtesy of Robert Hale Ltd)

'And,' continued Doris in a low voice, 'he was doing something with it when it went off. I think he was as much surprised as I was. When the maid came in I was seated and he was sitting in the chair opposite. Later he left the room and I went into the bedroom and put the gun under the mattress.' She then explained that the next day she was helping the maid clear up in the dining room when she saw a mark on the floor and so said to the maid, 'Oh that must be the spot where the shot went through.'

After Birkett had completed his examination, O'Sullivan rose to cross-examine. 'Who loaded the revolver after that first shot?' he asked.

'I don't know. I never saw it again.'

She said that she did not know how to load the revolver or where the cartridges were kept. When she had said that she wished the thing had been locked up, she meant the gun not the bureau.

'When you said that you were not fooling, you were pretty sure that the gun was loaded?'

'I was not. I meant that I wanted to know where he had been all night. I was not referring to the gun.' She insisted that her husband had said that it was loaded with blanks and that the blanks would not hurt anyone.

At this the judge chimed in. 'Then what did you mean by firing to one side?'

'I don't know.'

She repeated that it was not her who fired the revolver on the first occasion.

Re-examined by Birkett, she said that she was always terrified of having guns in the house. Her husband knew she was terrified and she believed that when he saw her with a gun in her hand it would be sufficient to make him scared. As soon as she returned with the revolver to the dining room he said it was only loaded with blanks. 'If he had never said that I would not have fired at all.'

When Birkett resumed his seat after his re-examination, Doris surprised the court by turning first to the judge and then to the jury saying, 'I would just like to say a few words ...' But before she could go any further, Justice Humphreys interrupted to say that if she had anything to say she had better inform her counsel, as he could not allow two speeches to the jury.

In his final speech, Birkett emphasised that the prosecution had raised the behaviour of the husband and portrayed it negatively, but Doris, when she went into the witness box, only said that she loved him and wanted him back. She had no sort of desire to hurt him. And when he wouldn't tell her where he had been, she tried to frighten him into telling her by producing the revolver. She never intended to fire it and when it did go off it was pointed not at him but to the side. 'If you study the evidence Mrs Teesdale has given,' he said, 'your duty in this case will be to return a clear verdict of "not guilty" on all charges.'

In O'Sullivan's final speech to the jury, he said that a person who deliberately took the life of any citizen, even with that citizen's consent, was guilty of murder. When Doris Teesdale fetched the gun it could be presumed that it was loaded and by her own confession she aimed a shot which she intended to pass between him and the table. He asked the jury to consider if this was not the determination of a jealous woman. Although she said she had no idea of using the gun, she changed her mind and fired it. On that evidence she should be convicted of at least the crime of manslaughter.

All the doors of the court were locked when Justice Humphreys began his summing up, with a strong warning against sympathy being permitted to enter the trial. He said it would be as wrong to convict the woman on insufficient evidence of murder because of sympathy for the relatives of the man who was killed, as it would be to find her not guilty because of sympathy for a woman who probably had a very good case for divorce. On the issue of whether she killed her husband unlawfully, the judge said there could not be the smallest question about it. The firing of a revolver in the neighbourhood of another person was most dangerous and unlawful. But the jury had to consider if the prosecution had proved to their satisfaction that when she fired the revolver she intended to kill her husband or hurt him. If they felt any reasonable doubt on the charge of murder they must acquit her, but they would then have to consider the other offence of manslaughter. 'I tell you quite frankly,' said the judge, 'that in my view as a lawyer, I cannot understand how you can fail to say that this woman is guilty of manslaughter.'

His summing up lasted an hour and a quarter and the jury retired at 1.15 p.m. The final scene in the court was enacted in an atmosphere tense with drama if not actual farce. The jury were out for two hours and ten minutes and when they had finished their deliberations they knocked on the door of the court to be let back in.

Unfortunately, another trial had begun in the courtroom. The judge was present but the counsels were absent and had to be hurriedly returned. There was already a new jury sitting in the jury box when the Teesdale jury filed in and they had to stand in front of the new jury members.

The clerk of the court asked: 'Do you find the prisoner Doris Vanda Ursula Teesdale guilty of murder?' And the reply came in ringing tones, 'Not Guilty!' The next enquiry, 'Do you find the prisoner guilty of manslaughter?' again received the reply, 'Not Guilty!' Doris Teesdale sagged forward against the dock rail and had to be supported by the female warders with her. There was applause in court, quickly suppressed by the judge, who then discharged the prisoner.

CASE THREE   1945

DISASTER AVERTED

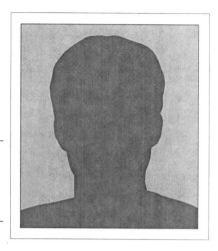

Suspect:	Thomas Ramshaw
Age:	49
Charge:	Murder

Thomas Henry Ramshaw was 49 years old. He was usually called Harry and he worked as a skip filler at John Lysaght's Steel Works, Scunthorpe, working the night shift from 10 p.m. until 6 a.m. He lived at Ravendale Street, near the High Street in Scunthorpe. Ravendale Street was made up mainly of residential terraced properties, although his house had a services canteen on one side of it and an optician's shop on the other. Beyond the backyard ran a wide alleyway known locally as a 'ten-foot'.

Harry Ramshaw had been born in his house and carried on living there after his parents died. He was looked after by his housekeeper, Emily Jane Charlesworth, who was a spinster of 69. She too had been born in Scunthorpe but had lived in Australia for many years as a nursemaid for a clergyman's family. When she returned to this country she became a housekeeper for Ramshaw and had lived with him for twenty-seven years. A devout woman, she worked tirelessly for the church and was quiet and unassuming.

Ramshaw normally stayed in bed for most of the day when he was on nightshift and on Saturday, 23 September 1945 Charlesworth called him at 8 p.m. to get ready for work. They had a cup of tea together and afterwards listened to the radio. When he left the house at 9.30 p.m. Charlesworth went with him to the front door. 'Goodnight Harry,' she said. 'Do be careful.' This referred to the ever-present risk of accidents at work, as he operated in the dangerous blast furnace area.

When he returned at about 6.30 a.m. on the Sunday, he found that the back door was unlocked. He called for Emily and went into the kitchen and was surprised to find the gaslight was still on, although it was by now fully daylight. He turned it off. Then he noticed that the kitchen table still had a cup and saucer on it, but others and plates were scattered about the floor. Puzzled, he turned and saw a sight that terrified him.

On the floor near the fireplace lay the body of Emily Charlesworth. She was fully clothed; she had obviously been attacked before she went to bed. Her clothes were soaked in blood and there was blood splashed upon the walls and the ceiling of the small room. But by far the worst was the condition of her face and head. Her face was unrecognisable from the savage blows it had received.

'there was blood splashed upon the walls and the ceiling'

Ramshaw rushed out screaming into the street. He saw the figure of a man he knew coming down the street. He was Ernest Dennis, who was an engine driver and was coming home from work. Ramshaw rushed up to him. 'My housekeeper's dead!' he shouted, 'Lying in the kitchen all covered in blood! What shall I do?'

'Is it a fit? Or did she faint?'

'She was all right when I left the night before! Tell me what to do.'

'Well, you'd better get a doctor. Are you sure she's dead?'

'There's blood all over and on her face.'

Dennis took Ramshaw by the arm. 'We'll go inside and have a look.'

When the engine driver went into the kitchen he was appalled. 'Are you sure it's her?' Ramshaw nodded dumbly. Like most people who had been living in the street for many years, Dennis knew a great deal about his neighbours. 'I think Miss Charlesworth has some nieces living nearby. You'd better get one of them to call a doctor and the police.'

Ramshaw rushed round to the nearest of his housekeeper's nieces, Florence Thompson who lived in Ethel Terrace, which was almost the next street along to Ravendale Street. He knocked loudly on her front door. She was still in bed, it being early on Sunday morning, but she heard his frantic banging and shouting and hurriedly got up and threw on

Ravendale Street today.

some clothes. When she opened the door he burst out with his story that Charlesworth was lying on the kitchen floor covered in blood. 'You get back to your home,' she said. 'I'll go and phone for a doctor.' With that she grabbed her outdoor coat and some shoes and set off for the nearest phone box. She rang up her local doctor, Dr Collins, and explained where her aunt lived and asked him to go there.

Meanwhile, Ramshaw had gone back to Ravendale Street to find that Ernest Dennis was still waiting outside the house. Ramshaw explained that the doctor would soon be coming and the two men began walking up and down. Next-door-but-one to Ramshaw lived Mrs Beatrice Foulston. She had heard the commotion going on outside while she was still in bed and had got up, put on some clothes and gone outside to see the two men walking up and down. She asked Ramshaw what was the matter. 'Something terrible has happened to my housekeeper,' he said.

'Can I help?' she asked.

'Yes, I'm afraid Emily has gone. Do you want to go round?'

She said that she would. But at that point the doctor came up in his car. And after being acquainted with the facts and the circumstances of the tragedy, he, together with Ramshaw, Dennis and Foulston, went to the back of the house and entered the kitchen that way. Dr Collins, after a quick examination of the body, said: 'I'm going for the police. I want everybody to leave and you, Mr Ramshaw, must not let anybody else into the house, is that clear?'

Next to come was a uniformed police officer, Police Constable Ogilvie. He went round the back and met Ramshaw coming out of the back door, crying bitterly. He explained what had happened and the constable went into the house and into the kitchen. In all his years on the force he had never seen anything like it. Charlesworth was lying by the fireplace and sticking to the curb by the blood was the woman's shoe, still buttoned as if it had been wrenched off. The constable went outside to talk to Ramshaw who confirmed what time he had left for work and returned. The constable then locked the house doors and went to report to his superiors. He returned with Detective Sergeant Kirby and other officers and they made a more thorough search of the crime scene.

Newlands Avenue today.

The dead woman was wearing stockings and there was blood on each of the knees. Her skirt was pulled up and her clothing disarranged, which made it look like a sex attack. Her dentures, both upper and lower, were on the carpet just above her head and a pair of spectacles was entangled in her hair. Under the table was a bent poker. A pair of fire tongs was propped up, upside down, in the fireplace and also in the fireplace was the handle of a brass shovel. A breadknife, bent almost in half, was also found on the floor. All these items were covered in blood. There was also broken crockery and knives and forks strewn about the floor. Also found was an empty Guinness bottle. The room looked as if a tornado had been through it.

Detective Sergeant Kirby then took a statement from Ramshaw. He said he clocked in at work between 9.50 p.m. and 10 p.m. and left work at 5.45 a.m. When he arrived at home he went in the back way, where the gate was partly open and the back door closed, but not locked. This rather surprised him, as it was Charlsworth's practice to be always up waiting for him to come home and to open the door when she heard him. He opened the door and called, 'Emily'. But there was no answer. He walked into the kitchen and found her on the floor. She had been alone when he left her and, as far as he knew, she wasn't expecting anyone to call.

The inquest opened on Monday, 24 September. The coroner, Mr Eric Dyson, was told by Superintendent R.F. Knowler, who was in charge of the case, that it might be some time before the police were able to present evidence. The coroner therefore only heard identification evidence from Ramshaw and Mrs Edna Warner, another of Charlsworth's nieces, who lived in Newlands Avenue. She had gone to the mortuary in Scunthorpe on the Sunday night, but was only able to identify her aunt by her clothes. Knowler also said that the chief constable, Mr R.H. Fookes, had asked for assistance from Scotland Yard and a number of officers had been sent, arriving on the Monday. They were Detective Chief Inspector Davis and Detective Sergeant Wolff, Chief Inspector Birch – a fingerprint expert – and Detective Inspector Law, a photographer. Through the coroner, the superintendent also appealed for information from the public. After this the coroner adjourned the inquest for a month.

The next day the police again appealed for information. They were anxious to trace a courting couple who were known to have been in the 'ten foot' behind the house between 9.30 p.m. and midnight on Saturday. The man was believed to have been a member of the Forces, but the girl was thought to have been local. The police emphasised that neither were implicated in the case and that the inquiries were completely confidential; they should not hesitate on any grounds to come forward and they might be able to give vital information.

The police also made an urgent appeal to customers of a local hotel to tell them of anyone they knew taking away a bottle of Guinness on Saturday night. The police considered that the bent bloodstained bread-knife may have been used by Charlesworth to defend herself, in which case the assailant may have been injured. They canvassed local hospitals to see if anyone had come in with any such injuries. They also emphasised that the ferocity of the attack had caused some alarm among local women that a homicidal maniac was on the loose, but there was no evidence to support such fears.

On the following Friday the police again made an appeal for the court-ing couple to come forward. They said that the couple may have felt that their evidence was not that important, but even negative evidence was useful because it could be used for verification purposes. It was also pos-sible that one or other of the two might have personal reasons for not coming forward, in which case they would accept evidence from just one. The police also said they would like to talk to a man with the following description: aged about 25 to 30, height about 1.75m (5 feet 9 inches), pale complexion and large eyes. He was seen wearing a khaki beret and a civilian raincoat with a khaki valise on his shoulder.

The next week saw some startling news. On Wednesday, 3 October, Harry Ramshaw appeared before Scunthorpe magistrate Mr J. Tomlinson, charged with the murder of Emily Charlesworth. Ramshaw, who appeared wearing a blue suit, was in a state of collapse in court and had to be sup-ported by two police officers. Superintendent Knowler outlined the case. The accused was questioned and had made a statement the day before, which would not be put in at that stage. Detective Sergeant Kirby related what had happened at 4 p.m. the previous day at the Scunthorpe police

Blast Furnace at Lysaghts works, 1945.
(Courtesy of North Lincolnshire Museum Service Image Archives)

station when, after cautioning the accused, he had told him he would be charged with the murder of Emily Charlesworth. Ramshaw had replied: 'I have told Inspector Davis all I know and that is the truth.'

The magistrate then addressed Ramshaw: 'You have heard what the witness, Inspector Davis, said. Do you wish to ask him any questions?'

Ramshaw replied, 'I do not know that I do.'

Knowler then asked for a remand in custody until 23 October. The chairman then asked Ramshaw if he would like to say anything and he replied, 'I do not want to be remanded at all.' The chairman then said that he was going to remand him and asked him if he had made any arrangements about applying for legal aid. Ramshaw said that he had not. There were tears in his eyes as he said this and he brushed them away with his hand. The magistrate then said that he would give Ramshaw a certificate for legal aid and he was led away by two police officers. The whole proceedings had lasted only seven minutes.

On Tuesday, 23 October, Ramshaw again appeared before the magistrates. Present was Alderman John Tomlinson, who was chairman, Mr D. Munroe,

Scotland Yard.

Councillor Mrs Ada Eyre, Alderman B. Holland and Mr C. Walsham. Mr J.F. Claxton prosecuted for the Director of Public Prosecutions and Mr T.J. Lewis, a local solicitor, represented Ramshaw. Claxton outlined the case against the accused and said that he had received a report from Professor J.M. Webster, a Home Office Pathologist, who had performed the post-mortem. Webster's conclusions were that Charlesworth had been relatively healthy in view of her age. There were gross injuries inflicted to her face; not a single bone of her face remained unbroken. The injuries to the face and head were caused by a sharp instrument and also by a blunt instrument. She had suffered manual strangulation and had received further injuries to her face and head after death. She had put up a fight for her life and the bruising on her hands and arms showed that she had tried to ward off the blows. Death was due to manual strangulation accelerated by the injuries to the face and head.

Evidence was also given by Dr H.S. Collins. He reported being called to the house in Ravendale Street at 7 a.m., viewing the body, calling in the police and telling Ramshaw not to let anybody in the house. On 28 September he examined Ramshaw, who had no signs of cuts, abrasions or bruising on his chest, forearms, arms, legs, head, face or hands. Cross-examined by Lewis, he said he would agree with Webster that Charlesworth had fought for her life and that it was possible the assailant would have some marks or injuries on him or her. Alderman Tomlinson asked, 'Can you give any indication of the possible time the woman died?'

'I would say about ten hours from the time I actually examined her, which was about 10 o'clock on Sunday morning.'

Lewis pursued his original point. 'Won't you agree that if there was a prolonged and desperate struggle, it is impossible to believe that the assailant would not have suffered some injuries which had left some mark on him or her?'

'Yes, I suppose so.'

Police Constable Ogilvie, who was the first policeman on the scene, said he was called to Ravendale Street by telephone at 7 a.m. on Sunday. He described going in the back way, seeing the body and speaking to Ramshaw, who had said that the yard gate was open and so was the back door with the key inside when he came home.

Vivian John Hunter, assistant manager of the Scunthorpe gas department, said that he had examined the gas meter at the Ravendale Street property and found that it would pass a small amount of gas without the insertion of coins.

Detective Chief Inspector Davis was next to the witness box and said that he came to Scunthorpe on Monday, 24 September. He went to the house the following Thursday and saw the dead woman's relatives there, with Ramshaw in conversation with Superintendent Knowler and D.C. Clarricoates. They told him that Charlesworth had a nephew in the RAF in India and another who was a sailor at Chatham. In reply to a question from Davis. Ramshaw said that Charlesworth always locked the back door before he went to work at night, but he could not remember if she locked up the previous Saturday night. Ramshaw then said that when he came home on the Sunday morning the gaslight was on, but going down, so he turned it out. He then looked down and saw Charlesworth was dead.

Davis said, 'I asked him how he could see her if the light was out.'

Ramshaw had replied, 'I could see her all right and it upset me so I ran and stopped a man in the street,' and then started to cry and said that he could not remember any more.

Davis said, 'I asked him why he didn't see a doctor who would give him a tonic,' but Ramshaw replied that he did not want to see a doctor; he wanted to get to work. He insisted that he could not remember any more and began to cry again.

This made Mr McGlone, a relative of the dead woman with whom Ramshaw was staying, say, 'Why Harry. You can remember what happened before Auntie's death. You want to be a man and not have the mind of a child.'

Davis continued:

On Monday, 1 October, I saw Ramshaw again and asked him further questions, but all he would say was, 'I cannot remember. I did not kill her.' I then suggested to Ramshaw that if we went to Ravendale Street it would probably assist his memory. We went there and Ramshaw showed me how he entered the house. He became very excited and kept saying, 'I left her in the best of spirits. I did not murder her. I did not even touch her.' I said that no one had said that he did. We left the house and as we were getting into the car Ramshaw became very agitated and said, 'I did not murder her. You are going to charge me.' I told him he was only being questioned. We went to the police station where Ramshaw made a statement. After he had made the statement he got into a police car to take him home and said, 'Shake hands sir. You have been very kind to me, but I did not do it.' We shook hands and I said to Ramshaw, 'I shall see you tomorrow after you have had a night's rest, as I still have a number of questions to ask you.' Ramshaw said, 'I wish it was all over and I could remember. I cannot remember touching her. I could not help it. I do not remember.'

The following day I saw Ramshaw again at 11.30 a.m. and told him I had further questions to ask him. Ramshaw said, 'I do not want to go down the line or get a life sentence for it. I cannot remember what I have done.' After he had been cautioned Ramshaw said he would write a statement down himself and said, 'I am sorry I done it and all the trouble that has been caused.' Ramshaw then wrote his statement, starting at 11.55 a.m. and finishing at 2.58 p.m., with a break for lunch from 1.30 p.m. to 2.00 p.m. After this he asked to leave, but was told he would be detained. He was detained, cautioned and charged.

The Oswald Hotel. (Courtesy of North Lincolnshire Museum Service Image Archives)

Detective Chief Inspector Davis then put in a statement alleged to have been made by Ramshaw. But Lewis objected on the grounds that they were not the free and voluntary statements of the accused.

Cross-examined by Lewis, Davis said that apart from the fact that Ramshaw was the last person to see Charlesworth alive and the first person to find her dead, he suspected him because he could have committed the murder. 'Also from my information, the body had been moved after the murder and not a single clue or fingerprint of the accused was found on the premises. This was strange to me seeing that the accused had lived on the premises for twenty-seven years.'

'Are you suggesting that the accused had removed all traces of fingerprints from every article in the living room after the crime?'

'I make no such suggestion.'

After further questioning, Davis agreed that the Guinness bottle found in the room had fingerprints on it but they were not those of the accused. And the landlord of the Oswald Hotel, where the bottle had come from, could not remember Ramshaw being in the hotel at any time. In addition, Davis was aware of a statement to the police by a woman who said that she had seen a light in an upstairs room at the house about 10 p.m. on the night of the murder.

Lewis pursued his argument: 'Were you informed of a man seen running up and down the ten foot at midnight on the night of the murder?'

'Yes, sir.'

'Have you found that man?'

'No, sir.'

'When you took Ramshaw to Ravendale Street, did you show him any photographs?'

'No, sir.'

'When did you show them to him?'

'When we were back at the station.'

'What did you show them to him for? They were not very nice photographs, were they? And some of them were quite gruesome.'

'I thought they would assist him.'

Finally, Davis agreed that the final statement Ramshaw had made was after he had been in the company of the detective chief inspector and Sergeant Wolff for ten hours.

The magistrates duly sent Thomas Henry Ramshaw for trial, which opened on Monday, 5 November at Lincoln Assizes before Mr Justice Denning. It turned out to be one of the most remarkable trials ever heard there. The prosecution was in the hands of Mr C.L. Henderson K.C. and Mr A.P. Marshall, and Ramshaw was defended by Mr Arthur Ward K.C. and Mr Walker K. Carter. Sir Alfred Thompson Denning had been appointed judge only days before, replacing Mr Justice Tucker who had presided at the trial of William Joyce and had recently been created a Lord of Appeal. There was a jury of twelve, all men. Three quarters of an hour before the court opened there was a queue outside the public entrance that stretched almost back to the gatehouse in the castle. And when the doors were opened the public gallery was filled to capacity within minutes.

When Henderson began the prosecution he said that a question arose in the case on which he wanted to address the court, but he thought it should be done in the absence of the jury.

The judge said, 'I have read the deposition. Is it to do with the admissibility of certain evidence?' Henderson said it was. Ward, defending, then said that he too was going to object most strongly to the evidence being given in court and agreed that the jury should be out of court. The jury then retired.

Henderson said that this evidence occasioned him great anxiety. He had received a report from the prison medical officer, where Ramshaw had been confined before the trial, and had shown this report to the defence. It showed that Ramshaw had an intelligence which was well below the average; in fact it was equivalent to a child of 11 and 3 months. Ward said he was going to object to the evidence given by Detective Chief Inspector Davis as he thought the situation might have had an effect on the accused that it would not have had on a normal adult.

Henderson resumed by saying that all the prisoner could say was: that he and Charlesworth had lived together for twenty-seven years on the most friendly terms, that she was a woman of great virtue and that he was the last known person to see her alive and the first known person to see her dead. Henderson said, 'Beyond that I do not see how I can put the case'. He also said the ceiling above and wall behind where this terrible affair took place were blood spattered, and yet Ramshaw had no bloodstains on him or his clothing. Some of the clothing might have been disposed of, but the possibility was negligible.

Henderson added that a bottle which came from a public house 100 yards away was found in the house, with no fingerprints of either Ramshaw or Charlesworth on it. In addition, a woman had seen a light on in an upstairs room twenty-five minutes after Ramshaw had gone to work. That room was Ramshaw's bedroom and it was reasonable to assume that Charlesworth had gone upstairs to make his bed. She had probably been disturbed either by someone knocking at the door or by hearing someone in the house. There was no gas in the bedroom but two candles were later found downstairs. It was clear that the woman had been murdered before she went to bed. It was a terrible crime and the responsibilities of the Crown were very heavy. But the Crown must prove its case and if he had to disregard the evidence of the detective chief inspector he would find it difficult to know what he could say, except that there was no evidence upon which a jury could convict.

Justice Denning said that for a confession to be admissible it must be free and voluntary and made without any inducement or menaces. 'Reading the disposition,' he said, 'I am quite satisfied that this confession is inadmissible as evidence against Ramshaw.'

The jury then returned to the jury box and Henderson briefly outlined the evidence he could put before them, omitting Davis' evidence:

The man who killed Miss Charlesworth was obviously a homicidal maniac and after he had made her unrecognisable and indescribable he then arranged her body as to suggest an indecent assault upon her. The prisoner has explained his movements and they cannot be challenged. The only thing against him was that he was the last known person to see Miss Charlesworth alive and the first known person to see her dead. I cannot ask you to find him guilty on this evidence.

The judge summed up, repeating much of what Henderson had already said and pointing out that Ramshaw had made a number of statements protesting his innocence. The only thing against him was the so-called confession. And he had held that it was inadmissible. The prosecution had offered no evidence. 'You have no alternative,' he said, 'and you must find this man not guilty.' The jury duly returned a not guilty verdict and Ramshaw was discharged.

As far as I am aware no one else was charged with the murder and it must therefore count as one of Scunthorpe's unsolved crimes.

CASE FOUR   1953

STRANGE MOTHER LOVE

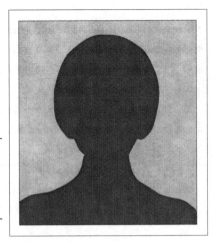

Suspect: Eva Williamson
Age: 40
Crime: Murder

'Lorna is dead! Lying in a pool of blood!' The anguished shouts of Harry Williamson echoed around the quiet street in Scunthorpe at about 4.30 p.m. on 1 September 1953. A dishevelled and blood-spattered figure had burst out of his house in Highcliff Gardens and staggered into the street, shouting and screaming and waving his arms about. He almost collapsed onto the pavement but shook himself and looked

'Lorna is dead! Lying in a pool of blood!'

around wildly as if wondering where he was and what he was doing. His shouts soon brought people out onto their doorsteps. One woman came up to him and asked what the matter was, but he shrugged her off. 'I must get a doctor! I must get a doctor!', not realising perhaps that if Lorna was dead there was little need for a doctor. He looked at the woman as if seeing her for the first time. 'The Thomases have a phone,' he muttered.

Luckily the Thomases only lived a few doors down and Harry staggered over to their house, closely followed by the woman who had come up to him. He knocked on the door and used their phone to call a Dr Yager who lived at Oswald Road, Scunthorpe. After a few minutes of incoherent conversation, the doctor got the message and phoned the ambulance service.

He and the ambulance crew arrived at Highcliff Gardens a few minutes later and entered the house.

Huddled in the corner of the living room was the body of a young girl. There was blood all over her body, but most of it seemed to be concentrated on her head, which looked severely battered. There was blood on the walls and even on the ceiling and the room was in a considerable state of disorder. The ambulance men rapidly got in touch with the police who soon arrived and reinforcements were called for. Subsequently senior officers, including Superintendent R.F. Knowler, came to the crime scene and Knowler was put in charge of the investigation. It was plainly murder.

Dr Yager confirmed that death had taken place at least two hours before and Harry Williamson said that the body was that of his 14-year-old daughter Lorna Judith Williamson.

In cases like this, the police must first look at the family for possible suspects. Harry was covered in blood himself and he had been the one to find the body. He inevitably came under suspicion. But he was quickly eliminated; he was a paint sprayer at the Appleby-Frodingham steelworks, had been at work all day and had only arrived home when he finished work at 4.30 p.m.

But where was Mrs Williamson? Had she been attacked and possibly abducted? And had the child been murdered in an attempt to protect her mother? The police had to consider all these possibilities. A search of the premises, however, turned up objects that threw a different light on the situation. In the backyard the police found a bucket and in it was a bloodstained chopper. And in a small gas copper in the washhouse they discovered some stockings which, when they were unravelled, were found to be bloodstained. Although the blood had yet to be tested to prove that it was young Lorna's, the finding of it was decidedly suspicious. The crime looked domestic.

An immediate search began for Eva Williamson, 40, the mother of young Lorna. The police force of the entire division was immediately mobilised and off-duty men were called back into service to assist in the search. Eight officers wearing rubber boots and carrying long staves searched the Hempdykes, an uncultivated escarpment, just to the back of Highcliff Gardens. Plain-clothes patrols were maintained on all Scunthorpe's main streets and fleets of patrol cars with radio communication toured the Scunthorpe area.

Constables from outlying village stations were brought in to help with the search and two policemen kept a watch at Keadby Bridge.

The search continued throughout the night and in the morning Sergeant S. Barker of the Royal Army Veterinary Corps Dog School at Melton Mowbray arrived with some canines to help. He was initially worried that the rain which had occurred in the early morning might have destroyed part of any scent trail, or that the strong wind might have blown the scent about. But he set his dogs off. One dog took its scent from a blue jacket belonging to Eva and immediately rushed off through the back garden and along a wide pathway that ran behind the houses at the back, the path eventually going over the Hempdykes. The dog crossed the Doncaster Road and went along Kingsway to the new college. Then it circled some fields and returned to the college site, but lost the scent there. The dog started again from the Doncaster Road, going up Kingsway and then turning right down Brumby Wood Lane. It went through part of Brumby Woods, across the Scotter road, over a field of cut corn and again into the woodland then on to Brumby Grove Farm where the dog apparently lost the scent again. A second dog was introduced, but it too lost the

Oswald Road.

scent in Brumby Wood Lane. The first dog took over again and led the way yet again to Brumby Grove Farm. By this time it looked as if the farm and its environs might hold some clue. And indeed Mrs W. Proctor, wife of the foreman at the farm who lived nearby, said that the farm dogs had begun barking at about midnight on Tuesday. 'They do not usually bark unless somebody is in the yard,' she said. 'We shouted at them to keep quiet and we heard no more.' But a search of the farm and the surrounding area turned up nothing significant and the search there was abandoned.

The identification of the body as that of Lorna Judith Williamson was made on the Tuesday, at 8.35 p.m. She was identified by her maternal uncle, Leonard Berridge, a commercial traveller who lived in Pontefract but had been staying with his mother in Scunthorpe.

Lorna was born in Scunthorpe and had celebrated her 14th birthday the month before. She went to the Secondary Modern Girls School on Doncaster Road and had been about to begin her third year there. She had a pale complexion and always wore spectacles to school. She also suffered with asthma, which had hindered the progress of her studies in the past, but she had received treatment for the condition at an open-air school and it seemed to have a good effect. According to her headmistress, Mrs J.E. Humphreys, Lorna was a shy retiring girl who was also very nervous. She never had any close friends in class and always walked to and from school on her own. This was echoed by one of the school assistants who said that Lorna was a very nice girl, but very reserved. She rarely took part in any of the school activities out of school hours such as concerts and parties. But she had taken part in a Coronation Day trip to London only the last June, organised by the school to see the sights, presumably the Festival of Britain and the South Bank. And she had also gone on a trip to Western-super-Mare during the August Bank Holiday week. It was a Youth Fellowship Camp organised by the Scunthorpe Methodist Circuit and Lorna had gone to the camp with Mr and Mrs T. Pettinger, friends of her parents who lived in the same street. They had two daughters, Janet who was 15 and Ruth who was 13, and according to Mrs Pettinger Lorna immensely enjoyed being with girls of her own age for a while. At the time of Lorna's murder, Mrs Pettinger's two girls were on holiday in London and she said, 'It will be a great shock to them when they hear about the tragedy.'

While the search for Eva continued, the police issued an appeal for anyone who had information. They also issued a description of Eva: height about 5 feet 2–3 inches (1.57–1.60 metres), dark hair with a roll at the back, believed to be wearing a fawn double-breasted fitted coat, a light brown hat and brown shoes. Plenty of people did come forward and most of them were of the opinion that Eva Williamson was a most devoted mother. Lorna had not been a robust child and her health had been her mother's greatest worry for a long time; the state of her daughter's health seemed always to be uppermost in her mind. Another neighbour said she was such a kind-hearted woman and always willing to help others.

At 6.25 p.m. on Wednesday, 2 September, Detective Constable G. Bearpark of the Doncaster Borough Police was just leaving the police station when a woman came up the steps towards him. She seemed very agitated and had a newspaper in her hand. It was a copy of the *Scunthorpe Evening Telegraph* for that day and carried the headline on the front page: 'Search For Dead Child's Mother'. She thrust the

newspaper at Bearpark, 'I am this woman you've been looking for. I murdered her.' The detective, when he had recovered from his surprise, led the woman into the police station in Doncaster. There she was questioned about what had happened and, after being cautioned, said, 'Well, I knew I had done it. Then I thought I hadn't. But she was with me at the time, so I must have done.'

The Scunthorpe Police were informed by telephone. When they heard the news Detective Inspector Leslie Kirby and two other police officers set off by car on the 28-mile journey to Doncaster. At 8.25 p.m. that night Kirby saw Eva Williamson at Doncaster police station, cautioned

Lorna Williamson.
(Courtesy of John Young)

her and she then made a short statement. She was then charged with her daughter's murder.

In the car going back to Scunthorpe, Eva became quite talkative; she talked about her life at home with her husband and daughter. She also said that she had changed her clothes before leaving home on that fateful day and put them away quite normally. She said: 'It is a relief to let it all pour out.' At Scunthorpe police station she said, 'I shall be glad when it is all over. All I want to do is to tell the truth. It's no good if I don't.'

Inspector Kirby also questioned her about 'salts of lemon'. He said that he had found a packet at her house and asked if she had taken any or had she any secreted on her person. 'No,' she said, 'I was going to take some, but I didn't.'

'Have you any on you?' persisted the inspector.

'No. I know what you mean. I shan't do anything. I have a bottle of ammonia which I was going to take, but I didn't.'

'Salts of lemon' is a misnomer, since it has nothing to do with lemons. Its chemical name is potassium hydrogen oxalate and one of its other names is 'salts of sorrel', for it is found in sorrel. It is also found in rhubarb. It has been used in photography, marble grinding, to remove ink stains and often in the olden days as a kitchen-cleaning agent. It also appears in an episode of the television series *Downton Abbey*, where one of the servants gives a pot of it to a footman to take upstairs for the family's meal, but then realises her mistake and replaces the pot for the correct one. It is strongly irritating to the eyes and the gastrointestinal tract and large amounts of it can cause cardiac failure and death. But the lethal dose for most oxalates is usually about 10 grams for an average person, though less than that for a child and small doses can kill little animals. So as a poison it is not very effective.

The inquest on Lorna Williamson took place at the Scunthorpe Hospital on Thursday, 3 September, with coroner Mr Eric Dyson sitting with a jury. Dr Robert Yager gave evidence as to the time of death and said that he was present at the post-mortem examination carried out by Dr David Hamilton Fulton, the Home Office Pathologist, early on Wednesday. He went on, 'After consultation with him I am of the opinion that the cause of death was severe brain injuries due to multiple fractures of the skull.'

Appleby-Frodingham Steelworks. (Courtesy of David Robinson)

Evidence was given by Kirby who said that Mrs Eva Rachel Williamson had been charged with the murder of her daughter. He was followed by Leonard Berridge of Church Bank, Pontefract, who said that Lorna was the only daughter of his sister Eva Williamson and Harry Williamson, and that he had identified her body at Highcliff Gardens on Tuesday. After the three witnesses had given evidence the coroner addressed the jury:

> That finishes the proceedings today. The law is that when I am informed that someone has been charged with murder, the inquest has to be adjoined after obtaining sufficient particulars to register the death. It will be adjourned to 2 December to enable criminal proceedings to be concluded and it is unlikely that you will be troubled anymore.

On the same day as the inquest, Eva made a three-minute appearance at Scunthorpe Magistrates' Court. She was smartly dressed in a fawn coat and hat and appeared composed. She sat in the dock accompanied by a uniformed policewoman. Harry Williamson sat to the left of her, just behind the dock. The only other occupant of the public benches was a woman in a black coat who sat in the back row with a shopping bag. Superintendent Knowler made a brief statement outlining the circumstances of the case and asked for a remand until Saturday, 12 September to allow further enquiries to take place. Eva was asked if she had anything to say and she replied in a low voice, 'May I have legal aid please?' The chairman of the magistrates said that this would be granted and Superintendent Knowler added, 'Mrs Williamson will be remanded to Manchester where she can have the medical attention she needs.'

Strangeways Prison in Manchester, where Eva Williamson was remanded, is one of the most famous prisons in the North of England. Built in 1869 to replace the old New Bailey Prison in Salford, it had a capacity of 1,000 inmates. It was built on the grounds of Strangeways Park and Gardens from which it took its name and the prison walls are rumoured to be 16 feet (4.88 metres) thick. The prison was originally open to both male and female prisoners, but in 1963 the facility became male only. But at the time of the Eva Williamson case it had one of the best medical facilities for women and this was the reason Eva was sent there.

She made another brief appearance at Scunthorpe Magistrates' Court on 12 September. She was in court before the magistrates and was able to have a few words with her husband and her brother, before being led into the dock by Chief Inspector J.C. Swaby. She was wearing a grey-green tweed coat and close-fitting fawn hat and she again sat in the dock with a policewoman. Superintendent Knowler told the chairman of

Eva Williamson.
(Courtesy of John Young)

the magistrates, Alderman Bernard Holland, that papers of a scientific nature were not yet complete and asked for a further remand until Monday, 21 September. Mr. W. Bains who appeared for Eva said, 'I have no objection to the remand,' and his defendant made no reply. Alderman Holland said that he hoped the matter would be cleared up quickly and Knowler replied that every effort was being made. But there was to be yet another remand on 21 September, this time for only three days, when Knowler said it then would be convenient for all concerned to proceed. Eva gave a half smile and nodded assent when the magistrate Holland asked if this was agreeable to her. She then left the box and, again followed by her husband, was led by the policewoman from the courtroom.

The committal proceedings, due to get under way on Thursday, 24 September, were again delayed. This time fog had held up the car bringing Eva from Strangeways Prison and the delay lasted half an hour. But at 10.33 a.m. she entered the courtroom and, accompanied by two policewomen, sat in the dock. She smiled at her husband who sat in the well of the court. Earlier, when the courtroom opened at 9.40 a.m., five women took seats on the public benches. By 10.30 a.m. some twenty people, most of them women with shopping baskets, were in the court.

Mr J.M. Evelyn, prosecuting on behalf of the Director of Public Prosecutions, outlined the case for the Crown and read out Eva Williamson's statement made in the Scunthorpe police station:

> I shouted Lorna to get up; I wanted her in the sunshine. But she didn't want to get up. I got her porridge ready, and then I put some 'salts of lemon' in it. She said it was nasty, so I took it away. I think I intended taking some so that we both could go together. Then I came to my senses and realised I didn't want her to go. I made her a nice breakfast and threw the other away. I think I put some in her tea but she was sick. I cannot remember what happened after that and then I came to my senses. I realised she was dying and I prayed for her to be at peace. Then I wanted to get away. I could hardly believe what I had done.

When she was charged and cautioned Eva Williamson said: 'I didn't mean to. I didn't want to leave her behind.'

Doncaster Road. (Courtesy of David Robinson)

She left the house in Highcliff Gardens and during the time she was away wrote and posted a number of cards. Two were read out in court. One read:

Please help Harry all you can. Let Lorna be with grandad Berridge if possible. [He died in 1944] I cannot understand why this had happened ... or what to say to Harry – he is so good. I want mother to know I could not help it.

This was sent to Mr Leonard Berridge, Eva Williamson's brother, and received by him at his mother's home in Scunthorpe.

The other read:

Dear Uncle Walter. Harry is in great trouble and need. Please do all you can to help him. His mother is ill too. They do need you so get in touch as soon as possible. All I can say now – Eva.

The first two witnesses were police officers who gave evidence of taking photographs and drawing plans of the living room, the crime scene, which were then shown to the jury. The next witness was Dr Yager, who described how he was called to the house in Highcliff Gardens at about 5 p.m. and saw Harry Williamson there. He had known the Williamsons for some time, being their regular doctor. He estimated that Lorna had been dead not less than three to four hours, and not more than twelve hours. Describing her injuries, he said there were five half-inch (1.27 centimetres) cuts on the face and forehead and two 'near punctures'. He believed that the girl's face had been washed after death. He was present when Dr Fulton made a post-mortem examination and later he conducted another post-mortem examination to ascertain if there was any evidence of poisoning. 'I found no such evidence,' Dr Yager said.

Dr David Hamilton Fulton, of the Home Office Forensic Science Laboratory in Nottingham, said he would class most of the cuts on the face and forehead as superficial, except for one: the left side of the skull was severely shattered. In his opinion, the cause of death was fracture of the skull and damage to the brain. He was shown a hatchet and agreed that some of the superficial cuts and bruises could have been caused by the top of it.

Miss Glenis Burrows, an assistant in the Scunthorpe Co-operative Society's Pharmacy in the High Street, said that about 3.50 p.m. on 31 August she sold an ounce of 'salts of lemon' priced at 6 pence to a woman. However, she could not afterwards identify Eva, although it was the only 'salts of lemon' she sold that day.

A baker's roundsman, Donald Stephenson, who was also employed by the Co-operative Society, said that he called at the house in Highcliff Gardens at 11 a.m. on 1 September. He knocked on the door and called out 'baker'. And he heard Eva say, 'Not today,' or something like that. She came halfway out into the scullery and her appearance was quite normal.

Passing the home of the Williamsons between 9 a.m. and 10.30 a.m., James Hutchinson saw Eva coming towards the house from the garden. Later on as he was again passing the house, this time at about 2 p.m., he saw that the living room curtains were closed. A neighbour of the Williamsons, Dorothy Nicholson, was waiting for a bus in Vivian Avenue at about 11.25 a.m. on that Tuesday morning. Eva Williamson came up and joined her. They chatted together and, as far as Mrs Nicholson could tell, Eva appeared quite ordinary. They boarded the bus together but did not sit together. Later that same morning, Mrs Erica Thomas, a teacher who lived at Highcliff Gardens and from where Harry Williamson telephoned later that afternoon, saw Eva Williamson in the Scunthorpe Public Library near the book returns counter. Eva smiled and waved at her, but they did not exchange any conversation.

It appears that Eva caught a bus into town that Tuesday morning and subsequently caught another to Doncaster. Certainly one of the postcards she posted that day was posted in Scunthorpe and the other, the one to a Walter Williamson who lived in Leeds, was posted in Doncaster. Walter later said in court that it was a great surprise to have received such a postcard.

Leonard Berridge next gave evidence at the committal proceedings and was questioned by Mr W. Bains, a solicitor representing Eva. He said that the Williamson family had spent the day with him at his home in Pontefract on 28 August and they appeared quite normal:

My sister has always been very fond of Lorna, devoted to her. She would be the last person who would want to do her any harm. As far as I am aware the Williamson family had been perfectly happy, but my sister has never been positively healthy – far from it!

He then went on to relate Eva's mental problems and afterwards said:

She returned home on 25 June this year and I have seen her every week since then. Her recovery has been nothing short of miraculous. I saw her last on 28 August and her condition did not appear to me have deteriorated, but she did seem very anxious.

He was followed by Detective Inspector Kirby who related the circumstances of her arrest in Doncaster, her transfer to Scunthorpe and the making of her statements. In reply to Bains, the inspector said that her statements were rambling rather than incoherent. She was fairly composed for the first half hour of the interview, but then broke down. Mr J.L. Fish, staff biologist at the Home Office Forensic Science Laboratory at Nottingham, said that he had examined both the axe and the stockings and found blood on each one. The blood was undoubtedly human but the samples were too small for him to determine which blood group they belonged to.

Entrance to HM Prison Strangeways. (Courtesy of Stemonitis)

Evelyn asked for a committal to the next assizes and Bains said that he would like to reserve the defence. The chairman of the magistrates, Alderman B. Holland, asked Eva if she would like to say anything in answer to the charge, give evidence or call any witnesses. She replied in a low voice, 'No. Thank you.'

Eva Williamson appeared at Lincoln Assizes on Monday, 2 November 1953. Mr R.C. Vaughan, appearing with Mr W.W. Stabb for the Crown, said a report had been handed to him from a medical officer at Strangeways Prison. This report made it quite plain that it needed to be decided under the Criminal Lunatics Act of 1800 whether Eva was unfit to plead. The jury had to enquire if she was able to follow the nature of the proceedings and understand them.

Dr George Cormack, Principal Medical Officer at Strangeways Prison, Manchester was called. He said that Eva Williamson was put under his care on 3 September and he had interviewed her several times and also received reports about her from his medical staff. He learned that a maternal great aunt had died in a mental hospital aged 86 and two cousins had committed suicide. Eva had had a successful business career before she was married in July 1936, and until 1952 the marriage had been a happy one. The previous October she had been admitted to the Bracebridge Heath Mental Hospital in Lincoln, and certified as being of unsound mind. She was there from 18 October until the middle of January and then she returned home. Later she went back and was transferred from there to another hospital in York called The Retreat. She returned home on 25 June. When she was first admitted to the Bracebridge Heath Hospital she was in a morbidly depressed condition and it was the same when she was readmitted. During her period at The Retreat she had delusions concerning the devil and evil spirits, but received a course of treatment there to which she responded very satisfactorily. She was thought to have improved and was discharged; although the prognosis was unfavourable the hospital thought she was ready to go home and her husband was prepared to accept her.

When Eva was admitted to prison she was morbidly depressed and detached. She seemed to have no idea that she had committed this very serious offence and did not seem to realise exactly what was happening. 'My opinion today,' the doctor went on, 'is that she is suffering from mental depressive insanity. She is certifiable as a person of unsound mind. I do not think she is able to understand the course of these proceedings.'

Answering Carter QC who was representing Eva, Cormack said that her husband had done everything he possibly could and had frequently visited his wife in hospital. Carter said that in such a case it was impossible for anyone to put forward a defence. He added, 'This poor woman after a happy and useful life has suddenly become stricken with this terrible mental trouble and now finds herself quite unfit to plead to this indictment.'

After a summing up by judge Justice Finnemore, the jury found Eva Williamson unfit to plead and she was ordered to be detained during Her Majesty's Pleasure.

The 'terrible mental trouble' is now known as bipolar disorder, formerly manic depression. It is characterised by episodes of a frenzied mood known as 'mania' with episodes of depression. Mania can occur at differed levels: at lower levels individuals may appear energetic, excitable and often highly productive, but as the level of mania increases erratic behaviour increases and people begin to lose touch with reality and exhibit very distorted beliefs about the world. This is a condition known as psychosis. With these episodes individuals are often at risk of harming themselves or others, and commitment to a psychiatric hospital may be necessary. Commonly these manic episodes alternate with periods of depression, which in severe cases may result in suicidal behaviour. It is thought that there may be a genetic link with the disease and so it may run in families.

Treatment these days seems to favour medication with lithium and recovery for the most severe cases appears to take from six weeks to two years, although a recurrence is always possible and in many cases likely.

CASE FIVE 1955

A NIGHT OUT WITH MENACES

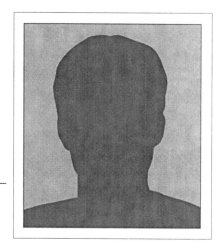

Suspect:	Kenneth Roberts
Age:	24
Crime:	Murder

'Well, where have you been at this hour?' Mrs Maureen Roberts' voice was high as she folded her arms and looked accusingly at her husband Kenneth. They were in the living room of their house at Spencer Avenue, Scunthorpe and her mother, Mrs Irene Craggs, was also in the room. It was 12.35 a.m. in the early morning of Wednesday, 11 May 1955. Kenneth Roberts, who was small and weakly looking with dark wavy hair, shuffled his feet and looked down at the floor.

'I've been to see my gran,' he muttered.

'What, at this time of night?' The pitch of her voice rose as she spoke.

'Yes, at this time of night!' shouted Kenneth and turned away to slump down on the settee.

Irene could see that this was going to develop into a row and she wanted no part of it. 'I'm going to bed,' she said abruptly. 'When you two come up don't forget to put the cat out.' This rather prosaic statement might have served to take some of the tension out of the situation, if not cause actual amusement. And it did at least result in a sudden silence.

'Goodnight mother,' said Maureen in a much lower voice as Irene went to the door. She looked down at her husband, who was sitting on the settee with his head in his hands, and wondered whether to continue the argument. It wasn't right for him to come home at this hour when she and her mother had been waiting up and worrying that something might have happened to him. And the explanation that he had been with his grandmother was plainly a lie; the old lady would not stay up that late. He did look upset, and possibly even contrite, but she didn't feel like making up with him at this stage. Not until he had told her what he had been up to.

'I'm going to bed,' she said. 'You can sleep down here on the sofa tonight.' And she went towards the door. But before she reached it she heard a sob from behind her. She turned and saw that Kenneth was rocking backwards and forwards on the settee with his face covered by his hands and it sounded as if he was crying. She hesitated for a moment. Was this another of his appeals for sympathy? Then she shook herself and stepped forward. 'What's the matter Ken?'

'Nothing,' came the muffled reply from beneath the hands.

Maureen sat down beside him. 'There obviously is something the matter, or it wouldn't have upset you so much.'

He shuffled away from her. 'Nothing's the matter! Go away!'

Maureen got to her feet. 'All right if you won't tell me. I'll go to bed.'

But this only caused a fresh burst of crying from the man. 'I've done something terrible!'

Maureen sat down beside him again and put her hand on his arm, since he wouldn't allow her to take his hand. 'It can't be all that bad. I know you feel now as if it's the end of the world. But you'll feel better tomorrow. And if you tell me about it now, you'll feel better now.'

'I've done something terrible!'

'I've killed a girl!'

'What, you mean you've knocked someone down on your bike?'

'No! I strangled her!'

Kenneth Roberts was 24 years old and his wife Maureen was 21. They had two children and were expecting a third. Kenneth worked as a warehouseman and their property was actually tenanted by John Fletcher, a steelworks loco driver, and Mrs Craggs was his housekeeper. The Roberts family lived in the house, but were on the waiting list for a council house. It must have been a considerable strain for all concerned, with four adults

Spencer Avenue today.

and two children sharing the house, but it was the fate of many families in those days due to an acute housing shortage. Fletcher was a kindly man who didn't mind sharing the house and was in some ways a father figure to the young couple. It was not surprising, therefore, that Maureen Roberts eventually decided to wake him and ask his advice. John Fletcher came down, where he saw Kenneth still sitting on the settee with his head in his hands.

'What's the matter old chap?'

'You'll have to get the police, John.'

'Why? What's it all about?'

'I strangled a girl in Winterton Road.'

John Fletcher pursed his lips. 'Have you been drinking?'

'I've had a couple of pints. That's all. I'm not drunk.'

The older man looked carefully at the younger. He didn't look drunk, but you could never tell with some people and he was making an incredible statement. 'Why don't you go to bed and sleep on it, Ken? See how you feel about it in the morning.'

'I'm not drunk I tell you! Why won't you believe me? I murdered a girl in a woodyard off Winterton Road! It's perfectly true!' And here he burst into tears again.

John Fletcher looked at Maureen. 'I suppose I'd better ring the police. Just in case he has. But they won't be very pleased if he hasn't.'

The call to the police was logged at 1.15 a.m. About ten minutes later, Inspector Evison and Sergeant Tyreman arrived in a police car. The inspector asked Kenneth to tell him what had happened and Kenneth replied that he had strangled a girl. After further questioning Kenneth agreed to show the officers where it had happened. In the police car going to the scene, Kenneth said that he did not know the girl. She had told him her name was Mary and said she lived in Winterton. She had asked him for 10s (50p in today's money) to get a taxi home.

Kenneth directed the officers to Mitchell's woodyard off the Winterton Road. When they got there he took them to a spot beside an old lorry near a dilapidated shed and there, beneath an old sofa, was the body of a girl. From her handbag found nearby, the police discovered that her name was Mary Georgina Roberts, but Kenneth Roberts claimed that she was no relation and this was afterwards confirmed to be true. Her parents were Mr Wilfred and Mrs Violet Roberts who lived at Roxby Road, Winterton. Mary was 18 and one of a family of seven. She had a married sister, two older brothers and three younger sisters: Silvia who was 16, Margaret, 14, and Joan who was 7. She was not married but was the mother of an 18-month-old boy called Peter. Her mother said that she lived for her son and spent most of her time looking after him. Until a month ago she had been employed for four months as a clerical assistant to the wholesale newsagent firm of Charles Henry Pickles of 2 Teale Street, Scunthorpe.

Kenneth Roberts.
(Courtesy of John Young)

Mary Roberts had blue eyes and fair hair and, judging by the photograph published in the newspapers at the time, was a very pretty girl. She had been born in Winteringham, but had been to school and lived most of her life in Winterton. Her mother said that Mary liked the pictures but would not go dancing; she had dates with several boys but had no steady boyfriend. Violet afterwards reported that her daughter went into Scunthorpe by the 3.30 p.m. bus on the afternoon of Tuesday, 10 May. She expected her back by the last bus at 10 p.m., but wasn't unduly worried when she didn't arrive, thinking she might get a taxi home or stay the night with friends in Scunthorpe. So she went to bed and was asleep when the police called at 3 a.m. to give her the terrible news.

Dr Russell Stanford of Frodingham Road was called to the woodyard at about 2.45 a.m. on the Wednesday. He certified the victim dead at the scene, but could not be certain how long she had been dead; he estimated only an hour or two.

Mary's father Wilfred, who was a pipe-fitter's mate, went to Scunthorpe Hospital to identify his daughter's body. He afterwards explained that his daughter was born with both hand and foot deformities; she only had two fingers on one hand and one on the other.

Stanford was present at the autopsy conducted by Home Office Pathologist Dr David Hamilton Fulton, who found that a blue chiffon scarf had been tightly wound round the girl's neck and secured with a reef knot. There was a deep groove and bruises on her neck and it was the pathologist's opinion that her death had been caused by strangulation with the blue chiffon scarf. Stanford agreed with this. He said that if manual strangulation had taken place there would have been fingermarks on the girl's neck, though he did add, 'I cannot be definite that death was not caused by manual strangulation, but there was no evidence [of] manual strangulation.' He also said that Mary was pregnant when she died.

The inquest opened the day after the death. The Scunthorpe District Coroner, Eric Dyson, heard four witnesses: Mary's parents, Dr Stanford and Inspector T. Evison. He then adjourned the inquest, telling the jury that criminal proceeding would take place and he would probably not need to call them again.

When Kenneth Roberts had taken the police officers to the woodyard he was then taken to Scunthorpe police station and charged with the murder of Mary Roberts. He said, 'I can only plead guilty,' and then made a statement, saying that he had drank two or three pints of beer at the Phoenix Club and left just before 11 p.m. on the Tuesday night. He collected his cycle and was preparing to push it home along Winterton Road and Half Mile Lane, since he had no lights. But outside the Phoenix Club he saw a girl standing underneath a lamppost on the other side of the road. She stepped into the road and asked if he would lend her the money for a taxi to Winterton, 'I've been let down by my boyfriend. We'd been to the pictures and then he said he was going for a drink. I waited for him but he didn't come back.'

Kenneth then said, 'It looks as if you've got to walk, so you might as well walk with me.'

They walked for a bit and then Kenneth said she again asked for money for a taxi and said she would let him have the money back if he lent it to her. Just then they came up to an opening at the side of the road and she said, 'I can make it worth your while.'

Kenneth replied: 'Where shall we go?'

She said, 'In here. There's a little shed and we can go in there.'

According to Kenneth's statement, they went in the little shed and she said he could do what he liked. They lay down and intimacy took place. She then got up and dressed and said, 'Well it is worth two pounds,' and then remarked that she had been there with other boyfriends.

His statement then went on, 'I did not give her any money and did not like what she said about other boyfriends. I just went crazy.'

To modern ears it doesn't sound very likely, but what is important is his description of what happened next:

I had been holding her with one arm behind her back and one on the front of her shoulder. I was holding her neck. She said, 'Be careful you might strangle me.' I said: 'Maybe that is what I intend to do.' I did so. I kept pressing until I could not hear her heart beating. She was wearing a scarf round her neck. I pulled it tight and then knotted it.'

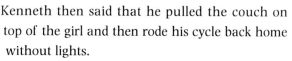

Kenneth then said that he pulled the couch on top of the girl and then rode his cycle back home without lights.

The funeral of Mary Roberts took place on the following Saturday at the cemetery in Winterton. A service was conducted in the little cemetery chapel by Revd E. Troup. Although it was a cold and windy day, many people from the village who had known Mary virtually all her life attended and there were many wreaths; one from a little blind boy bore the simple inscription 'With Love'. Mary's relatives stood around the grave for some time before they dispersed and Wilfred Roberts led his grieving wife away to the cemetery gates.

Mary Roberts.
(Courtesy of John Young)

The committal proceedings against Kenneth Roberts finally took place at a special Scunthorpe Magistrates' Court on Thursday, 9 June, Kenneth having been remanded three times in the preceding weeks. The chairman of the magistrates was Alderman B. Holland and the prosecution was in the hands of solicitor David Hopkin, while Kenneth was defended by local solicitor A.A Collins. A small crowd of people clustered outside the courtroom before the proceedings began, but when the court case opened the public gallery was only sparsely filled. Kenneth wore a dark grey suit but with a gaily coloured tie.

Hopkin outlined the prosecution case, describing how Kenneth left the Phoenix Club, met Mary and what subsequently happened, basing his account largely on what Kenneth had said in his statement. But Hopkin pointed out that the pathologist had said Mary's death was caused by asphyxiation due to the scarf being wound round her neck, in contrast to Kenneth's statement that he used manual pressure to kill her. He also said that Mary was a healthy girl apart from certain deformities and had been some ten weeks pregnant. Before the magistrates could commit Kenneth for trial, Hopkin pointed out, they must be satisfied that he actually killed the girl and that the killing was with malice, either expressed or implied.

He then called Dr Stamford and after him Mary's father, Wilfred Roberts. Mr Jessie Grist was then called. He was a labourer of Home Street, Scunthorpe, and had been in the Phoenix Club on the same night as the murder. He said that he knew Kenneth and saw him playing cards earlier in the evening; Kenneth appeared to have been drinking rather heavily when he came over to speak to him. A row broke out between the two men over something that had been said to Grist's mother by Kenneth's wife and her friends. Grist reported that Kenneth got quite angry, his face went white and his voice got quite loud. Later on, as he left the club, he saw Roberts with his bicycle. Hoping that Kenneth had by this time cooled down a bit, he called out, 'Goodnight Ken,' but never got an answer. He also saw Mary standing under a light across the road and saw Kenneth go across the road to speak to her.

After this Irene Craggs went into the witness box. After she had been examined by Hopkin she was cross-examined by Collins. In reply to his questions, she said that her daughter Maureen had two children and when Kenneth Roberts came home that Tuesday night he appeared quite normal.

Collins asked, 'Didn't Roberts tell you he had lost his head when the girl threatened to tell his wife?'

'No,' replied Irene.

John Fletcher next gave his evidence. He told of coming downstairs from his bedroom and seeing Roberts in a dazed condition, 'He told me, "It's serious Jack," and asked me to get the police, saying that he had strangled a girl. I suggested that he should sleep it off, but he said it was too serious.'

The pathologist next gave evidence, followed by Inspector T. Evison who described how he and Sergeant Tyreman went to the house at Spencer Avenue after receiving a telephone call and saw Kenneth who took them to the woodyard and showed them the body of Mary Roberts. He was afterwards taken to Scunthorpe police station where he was charged with her murder.

After a short discussion, the magistrates sent Kenneth for trial at the next Nottingham Assizes. Asked by the chairman of the magistrates if he had anything to say, Kenneth replied in a low voice, 'I do not wish to say anything at this stage.'

Kenneth Roberts went on trial at the Nottingham Assizes in the Shire Hall on Wednesday, 22 June 1955, before Justice Finnemore. The prosecution

Teale Street today.

was led by C.N. Shawcross Q.C. and Roberts was defended by E. Daly-Lewis. Shawcross stated that Mary Roberts was strangled after intercourse had taken place between her and a man. The case for the Crown was that Kenneth was that man and that he deliberately throttled her with intent to cause death. Shawcross then called a number of witnesses, including Irene Craggs. She said, among other things, that her daughter had recently moved into a council house with her two children. Answering questions from Daly-Lewis, she confirmed that her daughter was expecting a third child.

Wilfred Roberts gave evidence for only a few minutes, repeating what he had said at the committal proceedings, and was followed by Geoffrey Grist, who also repeated the evidence given at the previous proceedings. Inspector T. Evison was next. He repeated his evidence and was cross-examined by Mr Daly-Lewis, who said, 'You know that Roberts is not in good health? And has lost a number of employments because of it.'

The inspector replied, 'He has left sometimes of his own accord through ill health.'

'He failed to pass a medical examination for the steel works?' pressed Daly-Lewis.

'Yes,' replied the inspector.

'He was rejected as unfit for military service?'

Again the reply was, 'Yes.'

Daly-Lewis, addressing the jury of ten men and two women, said that he would call no evidence for the defence. He had a difficult task. In those days a murder trial was literally a life or death struggle, since the only penalty for being convicted of murder was the death penalty.

Two years after this trial, in 1957 a new Homicide Act came into force. For some years there had been moves in the country to get rid of the death penalty as in other European countries and the new Act was a compromise. If it could be shown that the crime had been committed in the furtherance of a felony, like stealing, or if a policeman had been killed, then it was Capital Murder and attracted the death penalty. If there was no act of a felony then it was Non Capital Murder and the sentence was Life Imprisonment. But this future Act was no good for Kenneth, who stood in danger of execution.

His counsel, after asking members of the jury to put out of their minds any feelings of sympathy (presumably for the victim and her family) went on to try and elicit sympathy for the accused. He pointed out that on the day before this terrible incident, Kenneth had been allotted a council house for him and his family to alleviate the difficulties of shared accommodation. He went on:

Whatever Roberts' intention, he placed his hands on the girl's throat and throttled her until her heart stopped beating. He panicked and then made a half-hearted attempt to conceal what he had done. This is the situation as I see it. Thinking as he must have done that the girl was dead; he tied the scarf round her neck when she was to him a lifeless corpse. For just a few minutes before he did that he had felt her heart stop beating. Roberts said he pressed with his hands until her heart stopped beating. Had he left her then she would still be alive today. My submission is that even if you are satisfied that he intended to murder the girl and that when he had his hands on her throat he attempted to do so, he must have thought when her heart stopped beating that she was dead. And what he did afterwards is not in my submission therefore murder.

Interior of the courthouse, Nottingham Assizes. (Courtesy of Nottingham Film Unit and www.picturethepast.org.uk)

The judge summed up for forty-five minutes. Referring to the defence's submission that when he tightened a scarf around the girl's neck, Kenneth thought she was dead, he said:

> May be this man attempted to murder this girl by strangling her with his hands and he thought he had done it, but he had not. The submission is that having thought he had done it, believing she was dead he tied the scarf around her neck and therefore he was not guilty of murder, but only manslaughter. You might find it extremely difficult to accept any contention of that sort. Did he deliberately strangle the girl, intending to kill her or cause her grievous bodily harm? If you find that he did deliberately strangle this girl intending to kill her, you will find him guilty of murder. If not, you will find him guilty of manslaughter. If the jury came to the view that the scarf was the only means of strangulation used, then the other point would not trouble them.

The jury retired for thirty-eight minutes before bringing in a verdict of guilty. Kenneth stood to hear the judge, who asked him if he had anything to say before sentence was passed. Roberts replied in a scarcely audible whisper, 'No, sir.' While the sentence was being pronounced he gripped the front of the dock until his hands went white.

Maureen Roberts had caught the early train from Scunthorpe that morning, leaving at 7 a.m. and arriving in Nottingham at 9.20 a.m. She went straight to the Assize Court and was able to see her husband for a few minutes. They were both tense to start with but Kenneth asked his wife how his children were and she told him they were well and happy. They were together for only a few minutes and then she went for a cup of coffee at a nearby café and afterwards went back to the Assize Court. There she met her mother and John Fletcher and together they went to sit in the public gallery. At the luncheon break Maureen again saw her husband and he told her, 'There is a lot to go through yet.'

When the jury retired, Roberts's solicitor advised Maureen to take a break outside and she did so, walking up and down in the street with her mother and John Fletcher. When she arrived back at the court the jury must have already delivered their verdict, for she said afterwards that she knew the result by the expression on the faces she saw outside the court-room: 'I was not building up my hopes on anything. I was just waiting for the result.' She also said she heard someone say, 'It is the worst.' 'After the result,' she said, 'I did not see my husband. I could have seen him, but I did not feel up to it.' After the verdict she sat with her mother in the entrance to the Shire Hall where the assizes took place, sobbing quietly. Collins drove her back to Scunthorpe.

Collins wrote a letter to the Home Office asking for a reprieve for his client and he received a letter on 9 July saying that, after a full consideration of Collins's representations and a consideration of the case, the Secretary of State regretted that he was unable to find sufficient grounds for advising Her Majesty to interfere with the due course of the law. The execution was set for Tuesday, 12 July at 9 a.m. at Lincoln Prison.

It was usual at the time for the executioner to arrive with his assistant on the afternoon of the day before the execution. He would report to the prison governor and would be told certain facts about the prisoner: his

Lincoln Prison.

weight, height, general build, etc. The executioner would also view the prisoner through a special spy hole in the door of the condemned cell, to satisfy himself that he knew all the relevant facts about the man or woman he was to execute. Then he had to work out the drop.

In olden days, prisoners were made to stand outside the Lincoln Castle walls in a cart drawn by a horse. A noose would be placed round their neck, secured to a cross beam overhead and the horse would be walked on, leaving the unfortunate felon swinging on the noose and slowly strangling to death. Later executions were moved to the top of the Cobb Hall tower in the castle and a gallows was used, but the effect was the same: the prisoner strangled to death. William Marwood, Lincolnshire's own executioner, changed all that. He used a carefully worked out series of drops and, by placing the noose knot under the right ear, when the prisoner fell the noose would swing round and break his neck, causing instantaneous death. All subsequent executioners in Britain followed the same procedure.

Kenneth's executioner set up his ropes the evening before and tied a sack on the end to represent the prisoner, which was left hanging all night to make sure the rope had stretched to its fullest extent. In the morning he would have entered the condemned cell and secured the prisoner's arms with a strap. Then the prisoner would be walked to the scaffold, followed by the prison governor, chaplain, prison doctor and several warders. He was positioned over the trap while the executioner's assistant secured his ankles with a strap. The executioner would place a white hood over the prisoner's head and then he would step back, remove the cotter pin holding the lever and release it. The trap would open and the prisoner would be launched into the hereafter.

In Kenneth Roberts's case the executioner was Stephen Wade. He was one of Britain's executioners from 1940 until 1955. He was born in Doncaster in 1887, but did not become an executioner until he was 55, assisting Albert Pierrepoint (Britain's most senior executioner) in an execution at Pentonville. He became chief executioner in 1946 and was often selected by the Sherriff of Yorkshire for work at Armley Prison in Leeds. His final execution was at Armley on 12 August 1955 when he hanged Alec Wilkinson for the murder of his mother-in-law, Clara Farrell, only a month after he had hanged Kenneth Roberts. His assistant in both cases was Robert Leslie Stewart. Stephen Wade died in December 1956.

On the morning of Tuesday, 12 July 1955 at just before 9 a.m., a group of people waited outside the gates of Lincoln Prison in Greetwell Road. They were mostly housewives and women on their way to go shopping or on their way to work. The distant chimes of a clock rang out and the group collectively gasped. Soon after this three prison warders came out of the small wicket gate in the massive prison doors. They carried a stepladder and a notice and this was nailed to the prison door and the crowd clustered round to read it. It announced that the execution of Kenneth Roberts had been carried out. A woman wiped tears from her eyes as the crowd slowly dispersed, but none of Roberts's relatives were outside the prison that morning.

In the same week that Kenneth Roberts was tried and sentenced to death, another prisoner suffered the same fate. This was Ruth Ellis, a much more famous murderer. Sentenced to death for the murder of her lover, all the national daily papers carried the story and a short piece appeared in the *Scunthorpe Evening Telegraph* and the *Grimsby Evening Telegraph*. Quite a furore erupted over the Ruth Ellis case and many efforts were made to save her from the gallows, but to no avail. It has been suggested that no reprieve was granted because a passer-by had been injured by one of the shots she fired at her lover, David Blakely. Ruth Ellis was hanged the day after Kenneth Roberts, at Holloway Prison by Albert Pierrepoint.

CASE SIX 1966

A QUESTION OF HONOUR

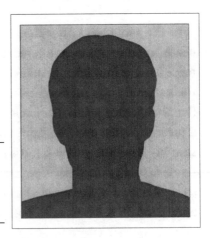

Suspect: Ahmed Yusuf
Age: 30
Charge: Murder

'You are just a queer and a woman as well!'

In 1966 this was an insult of the highest order. Homosexuality, even between consenting adults, was illegal and to accuse a man of being a homosexual was to degrade him. What made this even worse for the man being ridiculed was that the insult was delivered by a man who came from South Yemen, who were thought to have rather different notions of honour to their British fellows. He was 30-year-old Mohamed Mullahar Salih and he had a wife and four children who lived in Aden. The recipient was also from the Middle East: Ahmed Abdi Yusuf was 30 and from Somalia, just across the Gulf of Aden from South Yemen.

New immigrant groups, mainly from the Middle East, arrived in Scunthorpe in the late 1950s to work in the steelworks as the iron and steel industry expanded and there was not enough local labour to keep pace. Usually the men left their families behind and sent money home for their upkeep, which they earned from some of the more difficult and dangerous jobs in the steelworks, notably in the smelting plants. Mohamed Salih lived at Trafford Street and Ahmed Yusuf at Gurnell Street, both in Scunthorpe.

Yusuf replied to the slur by drawing a knife and springing at his tormentor. It was around 2 a.m. on Monday, during the night shift at the Appleby Frodingham Steelworks, which had started the previous Sunday night. Other steelworkers were surprised to see two of their fellow workers scuffling on the floor but, because they saw that one of them had a knife, they were reluctant to get involved. Salih managed to struggle free and staggered away bleeding profusely from stab wounds to the neck, hoping to make his escape down a flight of steel stairs. But he was quickly followed by Yusuf who came up behind and kicked him down the stairs. He then followed and continued to stab his victim who was now lying on the ground. Eventually he was hauled off his colleagues.

Salih was bleeding heavily. An ambulance was quickly called and the stricken man was carried off to the hospital. The police were also called

'staggered away bleeding profusely'

and Yusuf was arrested. A police officer saw a bloodstained knife lying on the floor near where Salih had been lying. He picked it up and Yusuf admitted that the knife was his.

Salih was taken to Scunthorpe's War Memorial Hospital. He was seen there by Dr Chacraverty who reported that the wounded man was in a

Trafford Street today.

severe state of shock, only semi-conscious and gasping for breath. He was immediately given a tracheotomy (an insertion into the neck to open the windpipe and to try and restore his breathing), but his condition deteriorated rapidly and he died at about 4 a.m. At a subsequent inquest, conducted by District Coroner A. Collins, the doctor said that death was due to shock, bleeding and asphyxia caused by stab wounds to the neck; a post-mortem revealed that he had suffered seven stab wounds. The formal identification of the body was made by Salih's brother Saed Mataher Salih, 36, who also was a steel worker but lived in Sheffield.

Meanwhile Yusuf had been taken to the police station and charged with felonious wounding. While he was in the cell later that Monday, he managed to injure his forehead and later the police became anxious about his mental state. A doctor was called and he advised that Yusuf be taken to a secure mental hospital. The nearest one was the Bracebridge Heath Mental Hospital near Lincoln and he was transferred there by ambulance. It was considered that as Yusuf had to be taken before magistrates the most convenient place to do this was in the nearby police station at Bracebridge Heath. And consequently at 10.55 a.m. the Scunthorpe magistrate, Arnold Machin, arrived at the police station with one of the clerks from the magistrates' court in Scunthorpe, Reginald Naughton. Soon after 11 a.m. Yusuf came from the hospital in a police van, handcuffed to a policeman whom he remained with throughout the proceedings. Chief Superintendent Kirby outlined the case against Yusuf, explaining about the self-inflicted wound and the transfer of the prisoner to the mental hospital. Yusuf was then remanded in custody. He was subsequently represented by solicitor R.A. Williamson who asked for legal aid and also for the services of an interpreter. He was eventually committed for trial on 10 May and subsequently received a term of imprisonment.

It was a tragic end to a few words spoken in malice.

CASE SEVEN 1971

A POLICEMAN'S LOT

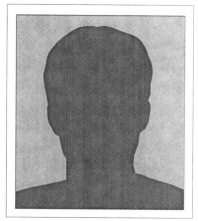

Suspect: PC Graham Wood

Age: 22

Charge: Murder

'Why, my front door's open!' said Police Constable Graham Wood as he got out of the police car outside the pleasant semi that was his home. It was early in the morning of Tuesday, 29 June 1971 and he had just come off a night shift. His home was one of the police houses in the Riddings Estate, Kirkby Road.

Police Constable Rogers, who had driven Wood home, also left the car as his friend started up the drive towards his house and called out, 'Could be a break-in, Graham?'

'That's what worries me.' Wood rushed up to the front door.

'Careful!' shouted his friend, 'Remember there could be fingerprints.'

Wood stopped as he was just going to push the door open with his hand. Then he nudged the door open with his foot and rushed inside once the door was fully open. He shouted in the hall, 'Glenis! Glenis! Are you all right?'

But there was no reply. Graham Wood stopped in the hall and turned to his friend. 'I don't want to make too much noise, because my 2-year-old daughter is probably asleep in the other bedroom. But I'm going up to see if Glenis is all right. You look around down here.'

Rogers nodded his head as Wood climbed the stairs. But soon there came a howl and Rogers raced up into a bedroom with the door standing open. Graham Wood was kneeling on the floor by the bed with his head in his hands and moaning loudly. His wife Glenis lay half in and half out of bed. There was something wrapped around the young woman's throat and her face was contorted. She had plainly been strangled.

Rogers rushed downstairs and out to the police car where he phoned for assistance. Senior police officers soon arrived. A police doctor was called in to establish that the 23-year-old woman was dead and a call went out to Dr Alan Usher, the Home Office Pathologist from Sheffield. Detective Chief Superintendent Miller Patrick, head of Scunthorpe's Criminal Investigation Department, took charge of the case. At first sight the bedroom looked disturbed, possibly by a burglar or thief looking for money or jewellery, and a careful search was made for fingerprints that could have come from an intruder. The house was also searched for other clues.

Police reinforcements, including the so-called commando squad, were called in from Grimsby and Lincoln and a full-scale search was made of the area, including gardens and outhouses, for anything which could help to find out who had killed the wife of a serving officer. The police obviously make every effort to find perpetrators of murder, but it is quite understandable that they would be especially keen to catch the murderer of a police officer or an officer's near relative. Detective Chief Inspector R.A. Smith was in charge of the house-to-house enquires and the Chief Constable of Lincolnshire, Mr George Terry, was soon on the scene. By mid-morning a mobile police station was set up in the area to act as a command centre for the police operations and a police spokesman said, 'We are now treating this as a murder enquiry.'

A letter threatening Wood and his wife had been found in their bedroom, and when he was interviewed later that morning he admitted to receiving several threatening letters in the past few weeks. He didn't know who was sending them and he assumed that it was someone he had arrested in the past and who bore him a grudge. Then as a matter of form he was asked to account for his movements on the night and early morning of the murder. He said that he had asked for a beat that night in the Ashby area as there were some enquiries he wanted to pursue there. Later that night, control lost contact with him as his radio was not functioning properly. Then, when it came back on, he asked to be picked up and went for some refreshments before getting a lift home by his friend Rogers.

An inquest was held and Dr Alan Usher, who had carried out the post-mortem, told the coroner, Alan Collins, that the death of Glenis Wood had been due asphyxiation, caused by strangulation with the flex of an electric kettle. He also said that she was pregnant. Identification was made by Wood's brother, Sergeant John Cooper.

But something didn't seem quite right to the officers examining the scene; it looked as if it had been staged. And then they heard a rumour that Graham Wood had a girlfriend. Not only that, but she was a policewoman and he had been to see her on the night his wife had died. Wood was questioned about this during the afternoon and after some time of denying everything he eventually confessed that he had seen the policewoman that evening. From then it was only a short time before he confessed to the whole crime. He said that he had asked for the night beat in Ashby because he wanted to be near his girlfriend. He had left her a note stuck on his car when he was in the police club. She later picked him up and they went to her flat for coffee. They had talked about his obtaining a divorce. Later, he went home and killed Glenis, pretending that his radio was out of order. Finally he turned it back on, was found and taken for some refreshments.

Police Constable Graham Wood was charged with the murder of his wife. There were a number of remands spread over several weeks but he eventually went to trial at the Leicester Assizes on Tuesday, 2 November 1971, before Justice Bristow. When the charge was read out to him in court he answered, 'Guilty, my lord,' in a low voice. Edwin Jowitt, who was prosecuting, said there was no suspicion that the woman Woods had seen that night (she had by this time resigned from the force) had any connection with the murder itself. Wood had previously spoken, Jowitt continued, of receiving anonymous threatening letters to lay the foundation that when the murder was committed it would look as if someone bore him a grudge. After leaving the woman's flat he went home and strangled his wife with the flex. There was no suggestion of a quarrel and it appeared that Wood went home with the express intention of murdering his wife. Jowitt then went on to detail Wood's further movements on that night and early in the morning.

Charles McCullough, defending, said that despite being a police officer Wood was very immature. If he had not done what he had done he would today have a wife and a daughter and a son of six weeks and he would still be a police constable. Jailing Wood, Justice Bristow said:

> The sentence that the law requires me to pass is one of imprisonment for life. Although this is not as bad a murder as one can imagine I do not think it would be in the public interest to recommend a minimum sentence.

LETHAL TRIANGLE

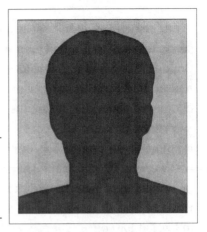

Suspect:	Dymitre Dembizky
Age:	Unknown
Charge:	Murder

The quiet streets of Crosby exploded into life on the last day of August 1971. It was a Tuesday and at 4.37 a.m. the police received a 999 call telling them a woman was being attacked in a ten foot behind a house in Burke Street. When the police reached the alleyway they found the body of a woman lying in a pool of blood. A little over half an hour after the 4.37 a.m. call, at 5.15 a.m., the police received another report – this time of a man attacked with a knife in a house in Grosvenor Street.

'lying in a pool of blood'

His name was Iwan Sarneckyz and he was a 47-year-old Ukrainian who was working in the steelworks. He had been divorced from his wife Maria since the previous October. They had both suffered a tragedy when their son Stephen, who also worked in the steelworks, had been badly gassed at work and died; his funeral had taken place only three weeks before. And now Iwan was lying bleeding on the floor. An ambulance was called and he was taken to the hospital where he died.

Meanwhile the police investigating the attack on the woman in the ten-foot behind Burke Street had also called for an ambulance and she too was taken to hospital where she died. She was later identified as Margaret Ann Dembizky. The police also received information that the attack on the woman had been witnessed and the attacker was thought to be the woman's husband, Dymitre Dembizky, commonly known as Frank. They lived at Burke Street, and the ten-foot where Margaret had been found was behind their house. When police entered the building they were confronted with a dishevelled and distraught man standing at the top of the stairs with a knife in each hand. There were three young children in the house. The police were placed in the difficult position of persuading the man, who turned out to be Frank, to come quietly for the safety of the children. But he was obviously in a state that he would not calm down. Waving the knives about and shouting that he would kill anyone who came near him, he was obviously a danger to himself and his children.

As dawn broke, the scene in Burke Street was one of intense police activity. Police cars lined the street, which had been sealed off at either end. An ambulance stood at the bottom end of Burke Street by the corner with Berkeley Street, and a crowd of several hundred people had gathered on the pavement to watch proceedings. In the ten-foot at the back, where the body of Margaret Dembizky had been found, bloodstains on

Burke Street today.

the ground were marked with yellow chalk. In nearby Grosvenor Street, a police sergeant and constable stood on guard outside the house where Iwan Sarneckyz had been found.

Meanwhile, in the property the vicar of St George's church, Reverend J.H.C. Laurence, climbed the stairs to try and reason with the disturbed man to at least let the young children go. But Frank was adamant that he would let no one go and if anyone came near him he would strike out with the knives. Later on in the morning, the Chief Constable of Lincolnshire George Terry, arrived to take charge of the operation. With him were officers from County Police Headquarters, including Detective Chief Superintendent Camamile, who was head of the county's Crime Investigation Department. They too went into the house to try and talk to Frank Dembizky, but were also unsuccessful.

Soon after, yellow riot shields appeared in the street and were passed over the front wall to officers who were in the front garden of the house. Next came police officers carrying collapsible ladders. These were taken round to the back of the house and assembled by policemen in the back

Grosvenor Street today.

Corner of Berkeley Street and Burke Street today.

garden. A red-and-white van next appeared in the street and from this police dogs were taken out and led round the back of the house. At 10 a.m. a uniformed policeman got out of a police car carrying canisters of what was believed to be tear gas. The assembled ladders were placed against the back of the house and at about 10.30 a.m. officers mounted the ladders. They included the assistant chief constable, Detective Chief Inspector R.A. Smith and Superintendent L. Hudson. When they reached the top windows they smashed the glass and forced their way in. Dembizky had come up to see what the noise was and the three officers grappled with him. But they could not hold him and he managed to scramble up into the false roof, still clutching his knives. Rather than chase him and risk serious injury, it was decided to introduce the dogs to the house. One of the police dogs, named Carlo, was let into the house and the three children found cowering in a bedroom were rescued and carried out of the house. The dog soon found the man and he was then secured by the police officers. He was covered in blood and had attempted to stab himself in the chest. He was brought out, his head covered with a blanket and taken to the waiting ambulance.

Ten foot behind Burke Street today.

The inquest on the two murder victims was opened the next day. The coroner was Mr A. Collins. Dr Alan Usher, the Home Office Pathologist from Sheffield, reported that Iwan Sarneckyz had suffered multiple stab wounds and had died from shock and loss of blood. Margaret Dembizky had been stabbed mainly in the chest and abdomen and she too had died as a result of the stab wounds. Detective Chief Inspector W. Felgate told the coroner that Frank Dembizky would be charged with the murder of both persons. At the moment he was in Scunthorpe General Hospital and his condition was said to be satisfactory.

But on 18 September, a couple of days before he was due to appear before the magistrates at the committal proceedings, he was found hanged in a hospital room at Lincoln Prison. So the mystery was never solved. Did Dembizky stab his wife because she was having an affair with Iwan Sarneckyz and did he kill the lover as well? Or was this just a domestic tragedy which resulted in him murdering his wife and he had nothing to do with the second death? We shall never know.

CASE NINE 1973

A CONTINUING MYSTERY

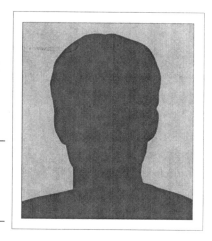

Suspect: Unknown
Age: Unknown
Charge: Murder

The Christine Markham case is one of the most famous in the annals of crime. It is also one of the most tragic. It began prosaically enough on a cool Monday morning in May 1973, with a mother getting three of her children ready for school. There was Susan Markham who was 13; Wayne, 10 and Christine, 9. Mrs Margery Markham was 36, and lived at Robinson Road, Scunthorpe. She waved her three children off at 8.45 a.m., little knowing that she would never see one of them again.

'she would never see one of them again'

The arrangement was that all three would go to the bus stop in Avenue Vivian, where Susan and her brother Wayne would catch a bus for St Hugh's School. Nine-year-old Christine would then walk on to her own school, Henderson Avenue Junior School, often meeting some of her school friends on the way. It was only a fifteen-minute walk from Robinson Road to Henderson School, but the young girl never reached it. Perhaps she had decided to skip school; it was the day after her ninth birthday and her father, 62-year-old Sidney Markham, said that she did not want to go that day and she had played truant before. Because of this, Margery Markham was not unduly worried when her daughter did not turn up for her tea, but when it got to 7 and 8 p.m. she began to have misgivings and sent out three of her older children, Graham, Susan and Carole, to look for her. If she was playing with her friends surely she would be hungry by now? When the children returned without her she began contacting relatives and friends, but nobody had seen her this late in the day. Margery contacted the police at 9 p.m.

Between thirty and forty local residents organised themselves into search parties and, assisted by police dogs from the Scunthorpe Police, began hunting for the child. Throughout the night the police and volunteers searched Atkinson's Warren, an area of scrubland not far from where Christine lived, and police cars toured the area within a mile of her house. The next day, on 22 May, police teams arrived at Henderson Avenue Junior School to ask children if they had seen anything of the missing girl. Meanwhile a special operations room was being set up in Scunthorpe police station.

A description of Christine was issued the next day. She was described as 1.17 metres (3 feet 10 inches) tall, with ginger hair, brown eyes and a fresh complexion. When she disappeared she was wearing a red long-sleeved dress, brown shoes, red socks and a 'wet look' blue coat. Posters showing a picture of Christine and other information were put up round the town by police who also asked all householders in the area of Robinson Road to search their sheds and outhouses.

The following day, Wednesday, saw troops from Kirton Lindsey and airmen from RAF Swinderby called in to help with the search and just before 9 a.m. a convoy of Land Rovers, army lorries and buses arrived at Scunthorpe police station. They were from the 12 Light Air Defence

Christine Markham.
(Courtesy of John Young)

Regiment recently returned from service in Northern Ireland. Coach-loads of airmen arrived from RAF Swinderby an hour later. They were all briefed by Superintendent Geoffrey Waddington who was in charge of the search. Then they went out in the heavy drizzle to help the police, although the weather prevented the use of helicopters. Also called in was the underwater search team from Lincoln Police, whose frogmen searched ponds and lakes in the area.

A spokesman from the police said that their main fear was the young child had become trapped somewhere. The heavy rain on Monday night might have led her to take shelter sometime during the evening and somewhere where she couldn't get out. The spokesman continued:

> If she is trapped she will have had no food for forty-eight hours and fears for her health are growing as the search becomes more prolonged. If we are going to find her alive. It will have to be today.

The following day, Detective Chief Superintendent Miller B. Patrick, Head of Lincolnshire Crime Investigations Department and who had taken over the investigation, said that police were following up a report that Christine might have been given a lift in a passing petrol tanker. Police were told that two girls, one of them answering Christine's description, were seen to have been picked by a petrol tanker in Queensway at 11.30 a.m. on Tuesday. The tanker was white with a blue stripe and was seen heading in the direction of Doncaster. The second girl had long blonde hair, was wearing a white jumper with a red band around it and looked to be about 16. She was carrying a coat over her arm. The police tried to trace the driver of the tanker and contacted local oil refineries. They also checked the possibility that Christine might have tried to get to Norwich where her married sister, Heather Brown, lived. But subsequent enquires revealed that Brown had not seen Christine. The same day the Mayor of Scunthorpe, Councillor Fred Clarke, attended the daily briefing at the police station and afterwards joined in the search with the officers, making house-to-house enquiries.

On Friday, 6-year-old Melanie Markham set out from her home at 8.45 a.m., the same time as her older sister Christine had left on the Monday. She was dressed in similar clothes to those her sister had worn:

Henderson Avenue Junior School today.

a red long-sleeved dress, brown shoes and a 'wet look' blue coat. Also like Christine, she was accompanied by her older sister Susan and her brother Wayne as she walked from her home in Robinson Road to the bus stop in Avenue Vivian. Behind her walked Detective Sergeant Jean Dunk and in the road, following in a police car, was Sergeant Bill Murray. With a loud hailer system he repeated:

> The girl in front with the blue coat is Christine Markham's sister. She looks like the missing girl except that Christine has ginger hair, but she is wearing the same clothes that her sister was wearing when she disappeared last Monday morning. Have you seen Christine? If you have any information please contact us now.

There were no troops taking part in the search that Friday, but a RAF helicopter was called in for the third time. A hundred uniformed policemen were expected to complete the physical search of Scunthorpe that day and seventy detectives continued with their house-to-house enquires. The police reported that they had received over 200 telephone calls from the public in the last few days and all the information was now being sifted and collated.

Meanwhile, the police put up a large hoarding in Scunthorpe's new shopping precinct. On it there were five pictures of Christine and the words: 'Have you seen this girl? If so please tell the police.'

On Saturday the police renewed their appeal for the tanker driver to come forward. Detective Chief Superintendent Patrick said that if Christine had been given a lift the driver might be apprehensive about coming forward because of company regulations about not carrying passengers in the cab. 'I want to assure drivers that any who approach me will be treated in the strictest confidence.' He also added that the police wanted to trace anyone who travelled on a Lincolnshire Road Car bus, route 234, which left the bus station at 11.20 a.m. on Tuesday. This went along Lloyds Avenue, Glanville Avenue, and Malvern Road.

On the following Monday a party of police wearing masks and rubber boots and carrying picks and shovels began digging in a refuse tip near Burrigham Crossroads. For weeks, loads of rubble from the Park Ward Redevelopment Scheme had been dumped there. Christine lived in the Park Ward and police said that it was possible she might have somehow got into a skip and been dumped with the rubble on the refuse tip. They planned to excavate a section of the tip 2.75 metres (9 feet) high, 9.15 metres (30 feet) wide and 6.10 metres (20 feet) deep and they expected it would take eight hours. Enquiries continued all over the country for the tanker driver and Patrick said, 'If Christine has left Scunthorpe it is very unlikely that she left on her own. Someone else must have gone with her and that someone is now missing herself.' He appealed for anyone who knew of a 16-year-old girl who was missing to come forward.

The following day, police set up three checkpoints manned by uniformed policemen and detectives at Althorpe, Wrawby Top and Wrawby Village. Tanker drivers were shown pictures of Christine and asked if they had seen her or given a lift to any girl in the last few days and if they knew of any tanker driver who had. Police continued to search houses: going through outhouses and false roofs and anywhere a young girl might have hidden. A police spokesman said that they had met with no opposition from householders, who had been very co-operative. He pointed out that Christine had now been missing from her home for eight days and this was the longest that a 9-year-old girl had been missing in Lincolnshire.

Atkinson's Warren today.

Finally a Grimsby man came forward to say that he had given a lift to a blond girl from Grimsby to Scunthorpe, two days before Christine disappeared. She fitted the description the police had given of the second girl – about 17 years old, blonde and wearing a white jumper with a red band around the waist. She told the man that she wanted to get to Scunthorpe, where she was going to stay for a while. Then she thought that she might go on to the Intake District of Doncaster. After a period of investigation the police announced that they had traced the girl, she was actually a woman of 24, and she was working as a waitress in Great Yarmouth. She was interviewed and eliminated from their enquiries.

On Monday, 4 June, when Christine had been missing for fourteen days, police appealed for two women to come forward. They had been in a minivan that had broken down on the Ashby to Grimsby Road on Monday, 21 May, the day Christine went missing, and they might have seen the young girl. They described the driver of the van as about 34 years of age, 1.70 metres (5 feet 7 inches) to 1.73 metres (5 feet 8 inches) in height, medium build with dark brown to black hair and she had a north-eastern accent. She was wearing a navy blue jacket trimmed with white piping and flat shoes. The other woman was said to be about 28, with dark hair and wearing light clothes. The van was a mid-blue 1961–1962 model, had part of the front grill missing and with black quilted padding on the dashboard. The women had apparently been shopping in Sheffield when their van broke down at about 8.30 a.m. They called at a mechanic's house and asked if he could repair the vehicle. He did what he could to get the van back on the road, but it went away running on only three cylinders. Detective Chief Superintendent Patrick asked for the women to get in touch with him and said that garages in Grimsby, where the women were going, were being contacted. His appeal was echoed by the head of the Grimsby Crime Investigation Department, Detective Chief Inspector Ron Smith.

The day after the appeal for the two women, Patrick said that from the time that Christine disappeared on 21 May there had been thirty-three sightings of her, up until 11 p.m. He was convinced that when she first went missing she was going to visit her aunt, Joan Shadlock who lived in Grange Lane South, Ashby, as Christine had stopped a woman that morning to ask which bus she should catch to get to Grange Lane. The woman told her and gave her 5p for the fare. About this time Shadlock, who was on a bus travelling in the opposite direction, saw Christine from the bus window and realised that the young girl might be going to visit her – she had done so on two previous occasions on a Monday. Shadlock immediately got off the bus, but had to wait a considerable time for another going to Grange Lane. When she got home she found that Christine had been there and gone, in fact a neighbour who knew her had given the girl lunch. Such are the vagaries of fate; if Shadlock had been able to catch up with her niece this story might have had a happy ending. The police dispatched a team to Grange Lane South and made house-to-house enquires to see if anyone else had seen the girl.

The police also issued a breakdown of sightings of Christine on that Monday and asked if anyone could fill in the gaps.

8.45 a.m.	Left her home in Robinson Road. Soon afterwards seen at Henderson Avenue Circle.
9.10 a.m.	Seen near Old Show Ground.
9.30–10 a.m.	Seen at the junction of Avenue Vivian and Long Road, where a woman gave her 2d. Then seen at the junction of Cliff Gardens and Oswald Road.
10 a.m.	Seen sitting on a wall near St Hugh's church in Ashby Road. Then given 5d for her fare to Grange Lane South.
10.30 a.m.	Seen near Priory Hotel in Ashby Road.
1 p.m.	Seen in Theodore Road near the house where she used to live. Numerous sightings during the afternoon.
7.30 p.m.	Seen in Ferry Road near Sheffield Park.
11 p.m.	Sighted for the last time at the junction of Davy Avenue and Long Road.

The police also said that there had been sightings of Christine on the South Coast and in Scotland but, although they had been checked, so far none had been confirmed.

A new search began at Atkinson's Warren on Thursday, 7 June and 200 policemen were called in, including detachments from Grimsby and Lincoln. The 4.83 kilometre (3-mile) square area had been roped off and divided into sectors and groups of men carrying sticks or shovels moved through the thick undergrowth and grass probing the ground. Each group kept in touch by radio with a mobile police van that was on the site. Luckily the weather was fine and so the men could mostly work in shirtsleeves. A police spokesman said, 'Although the area has already been searched we want to make absolutely certain that it contains nothing that will help us in our enquiries.' The next day the police finished their search of Atkinson's Warren without finding any trace of the missing girl.

On the Friday, Christine Markham had been missing for nineteen days. The police announced a reward of £200 for information leading to her finding. The spokesman said:

> During the past fortnight a great many letters and phone calls have been received from people all over the country offering encouragement to the police and sympathy for the parents of the child. Such is the concern of people in Scunthorpe in particular that two private citizens, who wish to remain anonymous, have offered £100 each to anyone who provides information as to the present whereabouts of the missing child.

Patrick believed that someone was in a position to provide information about Christine's movements after 11 p.m. He also thought that information about Christine's movements between 7.30 p.m. and 11 p.m. that night may give some clue as to her whereabouts as no positive sightings of the girl had been given between those times.

Ashby Road, near Brumby Corner. (Courtesy of David Robinson)

On Monday, 11 June it was announced that, although the police were still following leads, the physical search for Christine was being called off and would not be continued unless further information was received. Soon after this, detectives announced that they were checking a possible connection with another disappearance which took place in April 1969, 240 kilometres (150 miles) away in Norfolk.

It was around 1.40 p.m. on Tuesday, 8 April 1969, that 13-year-old April Fabb left her home at Council Houses, Metton to visit her sister's house in Roughton, 2 or 3 kilometres (1 or 2 miles) away. Roughton is near Cromer in North Norfolk. Young April cycled, carrying a packet of cigarettes, 14d (5½p in new money) and a handkerchief in her saddlebag. She was planning to give the cigarettes to her brother-in-law as a birthday present. Just after 2 p.m. she was seen cycling along the country road towards Roughton. Shortly after this, two Ordinance Survey workers found her blue-and-white bicycle lying in a field. But there was no sign of April Fabb.

Despite an extensive police investigation, no trace of the young girl has ever been found and the reason for her disappearance remains a mystery. Because it happened in such a remote rural spot there were no sightings of her beyond 2 p.m. and the police strongly believed that she had been abducted by someone in a car, van or lorry. Many number plates of those vehicles seen near the scene of the crime were taken and these were consulted by officers from the Scunthorpe Police. The man who led the hunt for April, Detective Chief Superintendent Reginald Lester, Head of the Norfolk Crime Investigation Department, said they would be looking for any comparisons between the two cases.

At the time of the disappearance of Genette Tate in August 1978 (a 13-year-old girl who vanished while delivering newspapers), Norfolk Police pointed out to the Devon and Cornwall Police that there were strong similarities between the disappearance of April Fabb and Genette Tate. Both cases are still unsolved but no link has been established between them.

During the same week police reported consulting with officers of the Norfolk Constabulary. Scunthorpe Police said that they were anxious to trace the driver of a car parked in Atkinson's Warren on the night Christine Markham disappeared. Detective Chief Superintendent Patrick said it was possible that the occupants of the car were a courting couple and that any information received by the police would be dealt with in the strictest confidence. The car was believed to be a blue- or light-coloured Corsair 2000 which was parked 100 yards inside the Ferry Road entrance to the Warren. He said:

> For elimination purposes we would like to trace the male driver of the car parked in the Warren at some period between 9.30 p.m. and 11 p.m. The driver was spoken to by two neighbours from Robinson Road who were searching for Christine on the night of her disappearance. The driver may be able to give information as to whether he saw a girl answering Christine's description entering the Warren and whether there was any other vehicle in the Warren at the time.

By the Saturday of that week, however, the driver of the Corsair parked in the Warren on the night of Monday, 21 May had contacted the police and been eliminated from police enquiries.

By the following Monday, Christine Markham had been missing for four weeks. Police said that after the most intensive hunt in the history of the Lincolnshire Constabulary there was still no sign of the girl. But a team of officers was still continuing to sift information that had come in from the public during the month-long search. Holidaymakers were asked to keep an eye open for Christine on the beaches, at fun fairs and other places that might attract a young girl. At the Lincolnshire Show they displayed a colour photograph of the ginger-haired girl. The show attracted thousands of people from all over the county and from neighbouring counties, and it was hoped that the sight of the photograph would trigger someone's memory and lead to some useful information.

Nothing much happened for a week or so and then the police issued another appeal to the public. They wanted to trace a number of people. The first was a young girl similar to Christine who was seen in the entrance and on one of the platforms of the Scunthorpe Railway Station, between the hours of 10.45 a.m. and 11.54 a.m. When she was spoken to by a railway official she said she was going to Doncaster, but when the train for Doncaster left without her she changed her story and said she was waiting for an aunt. Patrick said, 'This girl may not have been Christine. If it was not her then we want the girl in question to get in touch with us for elimination purposes.'

The second person the police were looking for was another girl, between the ages of 9 and 11, who was seen with Christine at the Queensway Roundabout in Scunthorpe between 9.30 a.m. and 11 a.m. The girl was said to be about 1.37 metres (4 feet 6 inches) tall – a little bit taller than Christine – and was wearing a brown mackintosh. The police believed that Christine may have told her of her plans.

The third person was a man aged between 30 and 40, broadly built with dark hair. He picked up a ginger-haired girl wearing a red dress in a light grey Zodiac or Rover-type car in Spencer Avenue near its junction with Smith Street at about 5 p.m. on the day Christine disappeared.

Train station, Scunthorpe, 1967. (Courtesy of North Lincolnshire Museum Service Image Archive)

The car drove off in the direction of Ferry Road. Patrick said, 'This man may well have been picking up his daughter after school. In that case we would like to hear from him to eliminate him from our enquiries.'

The last person the police wanted to interview was a man about 26 to 30, with bushy hair and sideburns, wearing a blue suit. He was seen walking along the Doncaster Road, near the Goldfish Bowl restaurant, at about 12.15 a.m. on 22 May, the day after Christine disappeared. He had a ginger-haired girl with him and they both turned into Henderson Avenue.

Intensive police activity continued over the next few weeks. There were still masses of information to get through and enquiries still to be made. However after six months with no new leads to follow the enquiry was scaled down. Police reinforcements went back to their respective stations and the enormous task of checking and rechecking leads and information from the public was brought to an end. But the enquiry was never brought to an end. In 1994, when Robert Black was convicted of the kidnapping and murder of four girls between the ages of 5 and 11, kidnapping a fifth girl and the attempted kidnapping of a sixth, several police forces became interested in him as a possible suspect in further murders and disappearances. The Humberside Police Force was one and Black was interviewed about Christine Markham. However, Robert Black has never admitted to any other crimes.

In 2002 BBC News announced that Humberside Police were looking at possible links with the Joe Kappen case. During 1973, Kappen was thought to have lodged in the Gainsborough area and worked as a lorry driver in Scunthorpe. He originally became a suspect in the South Wales murders of Sandra Newton, Pauline Floyd and Geraldine Hughes in 1973, but was not charged and he died from cancer in 1990. His body was exhumed and DNA extracted from it implicated him in the murders. But the South Wales Police said that because he could not now stand trial it would not be possible to say that he definitely committed these crimes. And the evidence linking him with the Christine Markham case (of him having lodged in the Gainsborough area and worked as a lorry driver in Scunthorpe) was not conclusive either.

In 2006 BBC News gave the information that detectives from the Major Investigation Team were conducting a review into the disappearance of Christine Markham. Detective Superintendent Colin Andrews said:

I don't want to raise hopes that we are close to a breakthrough ... We are conducting the cold case review as a matter of routine. The incident is being transferred from a paper system into the HOLMES (Home Office Large Major Enquiry System) computer and the family have been made aware of the review. Christine is still classed as a missing person, but sadly is presumed dead. My team would like to hear from anyone who still has information about what happened to Christine, but for whatever reason has not come forward. It may be that someone who detectives have spoken to has kept something back, or would like to add something to what they have already said. Either way, let us be the judge of how important the information is. Former officers, now retired, who were involved in the search for Christine, have been consulted recently over their knowledge of the case. DNA has been taken from Christine's family to help officers identify her should she ever be found.

Detective Superintendent Christine Wilson opened the Christine Markham case files in May 2013 with *Scunthorpe Telegraph* reporter Richard Sharp for the first time, to talk about some of the potential breakthroughs. A new line of enquiry first emerged in 2006 when police received an anonymous letter saying that a relative of the letter writer had helped to dispose of evidence, relating to Christine's disappearance, which had been buried in woodland near Metheringham. In 2013 the possibility of a dig at the location was discussed and a scoping exercise of the woods carried out. However, after the exercise a decision was taken that a search was unlikely to uncover any new evidence. Wilson said:

> When people bury a body, they generally dig where it is easy, but where it was easy thirty years ago wouldn't be the same today. The area now has trees growing that were not there thirty years ago and ground levels will have changed.

There are quite a few theories as to what happened to Christine Markham. One is that she never left Scunthorpe at all, but during the torrential rain of that Monday night sought shelter in one of the many building sites that were present in the town. Somehow she fell and her body was not discovered and is now covered with a building that was subsequently erected on the site. Or she might have been attacked by a building worker and her body disposed of in a similar fashion. If she did leave Scunthorpe she might have been picked up and suffered the same fate as those many other young girls who have disappeared around the country and their bodies never found. But no theory can detract from the tragedy and suffering of the family who still do not know what happened to their little girl.

BIBLIOGRAPHY

Books

Armstrong, Elizabeth M., *An Industrial Island: A History of Scunthorpe*
 (Scunthorpe Borough Museum and Art Gallery, 1983)
Bardens, Dennis, *Lord Justice Birkett* (Robert Hale Ltd, 1962)
Bodin, F. and Cheinisse, C.F., *Poisons* (Weidenfeld and Nicolson, 1970)
Clarke, A.A., *The Groaning Gallows* (Arton Books, 1994)
Clarke, A.A., *Killers at Large* (Arton Books, 1996)
Curry, Alan S., *Poison Detection in Human Organs* (Charles C. Thomas, USA, 1963)
Humphreys, Travers, *Criminal Days* (Hodder and Stoughton, 1946)
Wade, Stephen, *Foul Deeds & Suspicious Deaths In & Around Scunthorpe*
 (Wharncliffe Books, 2005)

Newspapers

Grimsby Evening Telegraph
Hull Daily Mail
Lincolnshire Echo
Scunthorpe Evening Telegraph
The Epworth Bells

Also from The History Press

MURDER & CRIME

This series brings together numerous murderous tales from history. Featuring cases of infanticide, drowning, shooting and stabbing, amongst many other chilling killings, these well-illustrated and enthralling books will appeal to everyone interested in true crime and the shadier side of their hometown's past.

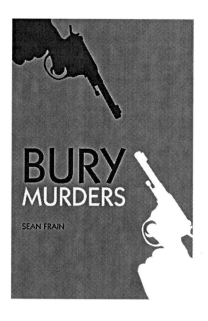

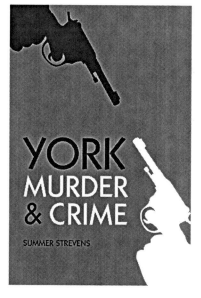

Find these titles and more at

www.thehistorypress.co.uk

Lightning Source UK Ltd.
Milton Keynes UK
UKOW04f1513061114

241227UK00001B/52/P

9 780750 955997